I0211135

MATHEMATICAL PUZZLES

and

OTHER CURIOSITIES

for

BRIGHT YOUNG MINDS

A COLLECTION TO ENTHUSE AND INSPIRE

STEVEN HODDER

TAKAHE PUBLISHING LTD.

2016

This edition published 2016 by:
Takahe Publishing Ltd.
Registered Office:
77 Earlsdon Street, Coventry CV5 6EL

Copyright ©Takahe Publishing Ltd. 2016
ISBN 978-1-908837-03-5

All rights reserved. This publication may not be reproduced, stored in a retrieval system or transmitted, in any form or by any means, electronic, mechanical, photocopying, recording or otherwise, without the prior permission of the publishers.

To Cameron Davis who provided the inspiration for this work

CONTENTS

8. Maps, Travel, Grid References, Longitude and Latitude

9. Mathematical Tricks

Chapter 1   Patterns, Sequences, and Strange Numbers

*This image has been generated by a computer using the mathematical concept of **fractals**. A fractal is a never ending pattern that is created by using some of the ideas introduced in this book: imaginary numbers and recursion. Fractal images can show an uncanny similarity to natural occurrences such as trees, coastlines, leaves and clouds.*

Patterns

When we start playing with numbers, we often notice patterns emerging. Sometimes, we are given a sequence of numbers and asked to complete the next few numbers by spotting a pattern (or the rule governing the sequence), for example:

What are the next three numbers in the following sequences?

> 124, 159, 194, 229, ...
> 7, 14, 28, 56, ...
> 3, 9, 27, 81, ...
> 256, 128, 64, 32, ...

Sometimes these patterns aren't always obvious. Can you continue the following sequences?

> 1, 3, 7, 15, ...
> A, M, J, J,...
> 11, 12, 1, 2, ...
> T, W, T, F, ...
> BBC, CDF, DFI, EHL, ...

If you managed to work out the last one, what might follow IPX?

Here's a pattern involving the number 9 with a challenge for you!
What is the missing calculation in this sequence of numbers?

$$12345679 \times 9 = 111111111$$
$$12345679 \times 18 = 222222222$$
$$12345679 \times 27 = 333333333$$
$$12345679 \times 36 = 444444444$$
?
$$12345679 \times 54 = 666666666$$
$$12345679 \times 63 = 777777777$$
$$12345679 \times 72 = 888888888$$
$$12345679 \times 81 = 999999999$$

Here's another pattern for you involving the number 8, remember the rule that you do the multiplication before the addition:

$1 \times 8 + 1 = 9$
$12 \times 8 + 2 = 98$
$123 \times 8 + 3 = 987$

Can you see the pattern and complete the table? Use a calculator to check your results.

Dividing

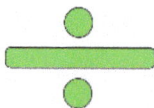

One number is said to be divisible by another if there is no remainder when we divide the first by the second e.g. 8 is divisible by 2 because $8 \div 2 = 4$ exactly.

Divisibility by 3

A number is divisible by 3 if the sum of its digits is divisible by 3

e.g.   12 is divisible by 3 because 1+2=3 and 3 ÷ 3 = 1 (no remainder)
        27 is divisible by 3 because 2+7=9 and 9 ÷ 3 = 3 (no remainder)
        20 is not divisible by 3 because 2+0=2 and 2 ÷ 3 = 0 (remainder 2)

What about 15, 26, 47, 57, 132, 744, 981, 1018, 1224, and 455682?

Divisibility by 4

To check if a number is divisible by 4, take the last two digits and if that two-digit number is divisible by 4, then so is the original e.g.

453926 is not divisible by 4 because 26 is not divisible by 4
732712 is divisible by 4 because 12 is divisible by 4

What about 988, 1024, 1582, 5660, 98832, 185462, 283756, and 26749328?

Divisibility by 9

At the end of this chapter, we present a little joke involving part of the nine times table. If we add the digits in each case, the total is 9 e.g. 2 x 9 = 18 giving 8 + 1, 3 x 9 = 27 giving 2 + 7, and so on.

A number is divisible by 9 if the sum of its digits is divisible by 9 e.g.

41 is not divisible by 9 because 4 + 1 = 5 and 5 is not divisible by 9
675 is divisible by 9 because 6 + 7 + 5 = 18 which is divisible by 9

What about 321, 531, 972, 5863, 78438, 105368, and 2687526?

Sequences

What are the missing numbers in the following sequence? Calculators are allowed!

9 x 9 + ? = 88
987 x 9 + 5 = 8888
? x 9 + 2 = 8888888

What is the missing calculation in this sequence of numbers?

1259 x 2 + 1 = 2519
839 x 3 + 2 = 2519
629 x 4 + 3 = 2519
503 x 5 + 4 = 2519
?
359 x 7 + 6 = 2519
314 x 8 + 7 = 2519
279 x 9 + 8 = 2519
251 x 10 + 9 = 2519

What are the missing numbers in the following sequence? (Calculators only allowed to check!)

76923 x 26 = 1999998
76923 x 39 = 2999997
76923 x 65 = ?
76923 x 104 = 7999992
76923 x 130 = ?

Cyclic numbers

Take the number 142,857 and try multiplying it by 1, 2, 3, 4, 5 and 6. What can you spot?

Think of the numbers being written on a strip of paper and the ends are glued together to form a ring:

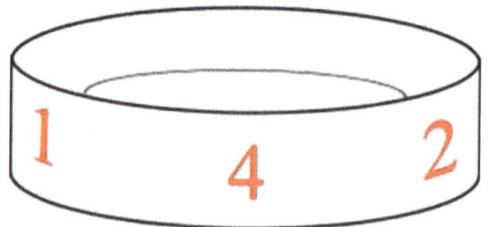

Vampire Numbers

Image courtesy of Wilsoninfo - Free Clipart and Animations

A *vampire number* is a number that can be written as a product of two numbers containing the same digits as the original numbers.

$$21 \times 60 = 1260$$
$$21 \times 87 = 1827$$
$$167 \times 701 = 117067$$
$$281 \times 443 = 124483$$
$$563 \times 953 = 536539$$

The pairs of numbers are known as **fangs**. Vampire numbers should have an even number of digits and each fang should be half that number of digits.

Other vampire numbers include 1530, 2187, and 6880. What are the fangs?

Some Famous Numbers

Some numbers are considered particularly significant usually because they occur naturally or that they feature in religion, history and mythology. We give a few examples below:

As we well know, there are 7 days in a week, but the number 7 is found elsewhere. In music, there are 7 notes in an octave: C, D, E, F, G, A, B also known by the names: DO, RE, MI, FA, SOL, LA, TI. The 7 deadly sins had their origins in the writings of a Greek theologian in the 4th century and are: pride, envy, anger, sloth, greed, gluttony, and lust. We also have Snow White and the Seven Dwarves, according to Shakespeare there are 7 ages of man, and there is the fictional spy James Bond, 007.

Apart from being the largest single digit in our number system, the number 9 also has some interesting connections. A cat is said to have 9 lives and if you are 'dressed up to the nines', it means that you are very smartly attired. Being 'on cloud nine' means that you are very happy. In Greek mythology, 9 daughters of Zeus, the god of the sky and thunder, were an inspiration of music and art. They were Calliope (epic poetry), Clio (history), Erato (lyric and love poetry), Euterpe (music), Melpomene (tragedy), Polymnia (sacred song), Terpsichore (dance), Thalia (comedy), and Urania (astronomy).

Our usual numbers are based on the number 10 and are referred to as decimal or denary numbers. The Prime Minister of Great Britain lives at number 10 Downing Street. According to the Bible, Moses received the two stone tablets containing the 10 commandments on Mount Sinai. The prefix 'deca' indicates 10 and occurs in such words as decade (10 years), decapods (creatures with 10 legs) and decathlon (a contest with 10 events). A 'tithe' is a tenth part of something usually in the context of a charge or tax, and a tithe barn was a storage facility for farm produce due to the church.

12 is sometimes called a 'dozen' which is related to 'dozenal' which describes a number system based upon 12 as opposed to our decimal system based upon 10. We used to have a complicated system of measurement that featured 12 inches to one foot and 12 old pence to a shilling. A day is divided into two lots of 12 hours and there are 12 months in a year. In the New Testament, Jesus had 12 disciples, Shakespeare wrote a play called 'Twelfth Night', and there are 12 people in a jury. The human body normally has 12 pairs of ribs, King Arthur's round table had 12 knights and there are 12 days of Christmas.
The French for 12 is douze.

13 is sometimes called a baker's dozen which is thought to have come from old English bakers who baked an extra loaf to their traditional dozen to avoid fines, or worse, for selling short measure. Perhaps this is why 13 is considered an unlucky number, although there are many theories. Many people avoid the number 13, some hotels don't have a room 13, and Friday 13th is considered a dangerous day. Such is the fear of the number 13 that a special term was created - triskaidekaphobia, which is certainly an impressive word! The number 13 appears quite often e.g. the number of cards in a suit, Rugby League is played with teams of 13 players, there are 13 stripes in the flag of USA, and the planet Neptune has thirteen known moons. Also, 13 is a prime number!

Questions

1. What can you find out about the following numbers: 40, 666
2. What are the 12 signs of the zodiac?
3. Who were King Arthur's 12 Knights of the Round Table?
4. Which dates relate to the 12 days of Christmas?
5. When you buy potatoes in a farm shop, they weigh them with an old pair of scales with weights used to balance that of the potatoes. Although they only have three weights, they can accurately weigh any whole number of kilograms from 1 kg to 13 kg. What three weights do they have?

Special Numbers

Some numbers are special in that they have some property that makes them rare or even unique. Sometimes it can be very difficult to prove some of these things, but it can be fun to discover some.

Many of these involve powers of numbers e.g. 10^6 is a shorthand way of writing 10 x 10 x 10 x 10 x 10 x 10 = 1,000,000. We talk of perfect squares and perfect cubes e.g. 9 is a perfect square because it is 3 x 3 (in other words, its square root is a whole number). 8 is an example of a perfect cube because it is 2 x 2 x 2, otherwise written 2^3. Any number raised to the power 1, is simply itself e.g. $6^1 = 6$.

89 and 135

89 and 135 are interesting numbers because $89 = 8^1 + 9^2$ and $135 = 1^1 + 3^2 + 5^3$.

There is another number between 170 and 180 that also has this property. Can you work out what it is it?

381654729

The number 381654729 is special because if you take its digits from the left hand side in groups of 1, 2, and 3 we can check the following:

3 is exactly divisible by 1 (obviously)
38 is exactly divisible by 2
381 is exactly divisible by 3 (did you remember the rule?)
Does this extend further?

22024

This has a "mirror image equality":

13×13 + 42×42 + 53×53 + 57×57 + 68×68 + 97×97 = 79×79 + 86×86 + 75×75 + 35×35 + 24×24 + 31×31

More curiosities involving the number 9

A nice trick involves Kaprekar's Sequence:

Ask a friend to think of a 2-digit number, (not repeated digits). Suppose they think of 47. Now ask them to reverse the digits of the number, so in our example, we get 74

Then ask them to subtract the smaller number from the larger (74 – 47 = 27)
The result is exactly divisible by 9.

Try this for yourself with various two-digit numbers.

Let's finish this chapter on a similar theme with a mathematical joke in which a boy has been asked some simple arithmetic questions. See next page for details.

```
1 X 9 =
2 X 9 =
3 X 9 =
4 X 9 =
5 X 9 =
6 X 9 =
7 x 9 =
8 X 9 =
9 X 9 =
```

He looks at the first one and says "That's easy, one times nine equals nine!" and he writes the answer in. He then looks at the next one and says "Two times nine, hmm, that's a bit tricky!" So he moves onto the next and can't do that one either. After another couple of questions that he can't answer, he says "There's a lot of questions that I can't answer. I wonder how many?" so he starts counting, writing down the number at each stage.

```
1 X 9 = 9
2 X 9 = 1
3 X 9 = 2
4 X 9 = 3
5 X 9 = 4
6 X 9 = 5
7 x 9 = 6
8 X 9 = 7
9 X 9 = 8
```

"Wow, eight questions that I can't do! That's impossible! I'd better check", he says, and repeats the count starting from the bottom. Again, he writes in the numbers as he counts.

```
1 X 9 = 9
2 X 9 = 1 8
3 X 9 = 2 7
4 X 9 = 3 6
5 X 9 = 4 5
6 X 9 = 5 4
7 x 9 = 6 3
8 X 9 = 7 2
9 X 9 = 8 1
```

"Bah!" he says, "I never could do arithmetic!"

That's all for this chapter, but we'll leave you with a few puzzles based upon some of the topics that we have covered so far.

FURTHER QUESTIONS

1. Can you find a 2-digit number that is sandwiched by a perfect square and a perfect cube? Note: this number was proved to be the only one of its kind by the great mathematician Pierre de Fermat.

2. Thinking about numbers being raised to a power e.g. 3^4 = 3x3x3x3 = 81, can you find values of x and y such that $x^y = y^x$?

3. Can you find a 2-digit number which, when you reverse its digits and then add or subtract the result from the original number, the result is a perfect square in each case?

4. Find the next two numbers in the following patterns:

   2, 6, 18, 54, ...
   1, 6, 16, 36, ...
   4, 3, 5, 2, 6, 1, ...
   1, 4, 9, 16, 25, ...
   31, 28, 31, 30, 31, ...

5. With the help of a calculator, write down the values of 1/7, 2/7, 3/7, ... , 6/7 using the first 6 digits after the decimal point. What do you notice? What would you call the number 1/7?

6. 1395 and 1435 are two more examples of *vampire numbers*. What are their fangs?

7. Calculate the value of $5^1 + 1^2 + 8^3$. What do you notice?

8. There is a number between 590 and 600 that also has this property. What is it?

9. The number 40 is written as FORTY. What's special about that?

10. A palindrome is a word that reads the same in both directions e.g. ROTOR. Similarly, we have palindromic numbers e.g. 34743. If we take any 2-digit number e.g. 47 and add the reverse of the same number (in this case 74) we get 121, a palindrome. If the result is not a palindrome repeat the procedure with the result. Eventually, you will get a palindrome. Try this with 69.

Answers to Questions for Chapter One

<u>Patterns</u>

124, 159, 194, 229, 264, 299, 334 (add 35 to the previous term)
7, 14, 28, 56, 112, 224, 448 (double the previous term)
3, 9, 27, 81, 243, 729, 2187 (triple the previous term)
256, 128, 64, 32, 16, 8, 4 (half the previous term)

1, 3, 7, 15, 31, 63, 127 (double the previous term and add 1)
A, M, J, J, A, S, O (months of the year)
11, 12, 1, 2, 3, 4, 5 (hours on a clock)
T, W, T, F, S, S, M (days of the week)
BBC, CDF, DFI, EHL, FJO, GLR, HNU (advance 1 from 1st letter, 2 from 2nd, 3 from 3rd)
Continuing this sequence we get IPX, but if we advance 3 from X, we go beyond the end of the alphabet! The normal procedure is to 'wrap around' and start again from 'A', so we get:
HNU, IPX, JRA

12345679 x 45 = 555555555

1 x 8 + 1 = 9
12 x 8 + 2 = 98
123 x 8 + 3 = 987
1234 x 8 + 4 = 9876
12345 x 8 + 5 = 98765
123456 x 8 + 6 = 987654
1234567 x 8 + 7 = 9876543
12345678 x 8 + 8 = 98765432
123456789 x 8 + 9 = 987654321

<u>Divisibility by 3</u>

15, 57, 132, 744, 981, 1224, and 455682 are divisible by 3
26, 47 and 1018 are not divisible by 3

<u>Divisibility by 4</u>

988, 1024, 5660, 98832, 283756, and 26749328 are divisible by 4
1582 and 185462 are not divisible by 4

Divisibility by 9

972, 531 and 2687526 are divisible by 9
321, 5863, 78438 and 105368 are not divisible by 9

Sequences

9 x 9 + 7 = 88
98 x 9 + 6 = 888
987 x 9 + 5 = 8888
9876 x 9 + 4 = 88888
98765 x 9 + 3 = 888888
987654 x 9 + 2 = 8888888
9876543 x 9 + 1 = 88888888

1259 x 2 + 1 = 2519
 839 x 3 + 2 = 2519
 629 x 4 + 3 = 2519
 503 x 5 + 4 = 2519
 419 x 6 + 5 = 2519
 359 x 7 + 6 = 2519
 314 x 8 + 7 = 2519
 279 x 9 + 8 = 2519
 251 x 10 + 9 = 2519

76923 x 26 = 1999998
76923 x 39 = 2999997
76923 x 52 = 3999996
76923 x 65 = 4999995
76923 x 78 = 5999994
76923 x 91 = 6999993
76923 x 104 = 7999992
76923 x 117 = 8999991
76923 x 130 = 9999990

Cyclic Numbers

142857 x 1 = 142857
142857 x 2 = 285714
142857 x 3 = 428571

142857 x 4 = 571428
142857 x 5 = 714285
142857 x 6 = 857142

Vampire Numbers

1530 = 51 x 30 so the fangs are 51 and 30
2187 = 21 x 87 so the fangs are 21 and 87
6880 = 86 x 80 so the fangs are 86 and 80

Famous Numbers

1. 40 occurs several times in the Bible e.g. it rained for 40 days and nights causing the flood when Noah sailed his ark, the Israelites spent 40 years in the wilderness. There are 40 days in Lent, corresponding to the 40 days Jesus spent fasting in the desert. 666 is the number of the beast!

2. The 12 signs of the zodiac: Aries (the ram), Taurus (the bull), Gemini (the twins), Cancer (the crab), Leo (the lion), Virgo (the maiden), Libra (the scales), Scorpio (the scorpion), Sagittarius (the archer), Capricorn (the goat), Aquarius (the water-bearer), Pisces (the fish).

3. King Arthur's 12 Knights of the Round Table: Lancelot, Gawain, Geraint, Percival, Bors the Younger, Lamorak, Kay, Gareth, Bedivere, Gaheris, Galahad, and Tristan.

4. The 12 days of Christmas: 25th December to the 5th January.

5. 1 kg, 3 kg and 9 kg. Remember that you can put a weight on the potato side, effectively creating a negative number!

Special Numbers

The number between 170 and 180 that is the sum of the squares of its digits is:
$175 = 1^1 + 7^2 + 5^3$

Answers to Further Questions

1. 26 is between 25 and 27 i.e. 5^2 and 3^3

2. x=4, y=2 giving $4^2 = 2^4$

3. 65 because $65 - 56 = 9 = 3^2$ and $65 + 56 = 121 = 11^2$

4. 2, 6, 18, 54, 162, 486 (multiply the previous number by 3)
    1, 6, 16, 36, 76, 156 (multiply by 2 then add 4)
    4, 3, 5, 2, 6, 1, 7, 0 (-1, +2, -3, +4, -5, +6, -7)
    1, 4, 9, 16, 25, 36, 49 (1^2, 2^2, 3^2, ...)
    31, 28, 31, 30, 31, 30, 31 (days in the months of a non-leap year)

5. 1/7 = 0.142857 using the first 6 digits after the decimal point.
    For 2/7 etc. the same 6 digits occur in a cyclic fashion.
    The number 1/7 is an example of a cyclic number

6. 1395 and 1435 are *vampire numbers* with fangs of 15, 93 and 35, 41

7. $5^1 + 1^2 + 8^3 = 518$

8. $5^1 + 9^2 + 8^3 = 598$

9. The letters of FORTY are in alphabetical order. It is the only such number.

10.   69 + 96 = 165
       165 + 561 = 726
       726 + 627 = 1353
       1353 + 3531 = 4884 (a palindrome)

    Note that the only 2-digit number that might be a problem is 89 (or 98) which
    requires 24 lots of addition before it reaches a palindrome!

Chapter 2   Numbers and their Representation

In the previous chapter, we looked at particular numbers with special names and properties. This chapter considers how numbers can be represented and some special types of numbers. Finally, we look at the mathematics associated with time and dates.

Binary Numbers

Binary numbers are a way of representing our normal numbers by just using 0s and 1s. The numbers that we use every day have the digits 0, 1, 2, 3 .... 9 and every number is made up of various digits multiplying some power of 10. For example:

$169 = 1 \times 100 + 6 \times 10 + 9 \times 1 = 1 \times 10^2 + 6 \times 10^1 + 9 \times 10^0$
Remember that any number to the power 0 is equal to 1.
$53724 = 5 \times 10,000 + 3 \times 1000 + 7 \times 100 + 2 \times 10 + 4 \times 1 = 5 \times 10^4 + 3 \times 10^3 + 7 \times 10^2 + 2 \times 10^1 + 4 \times 10^0$

In binary, we only have the digits 0 and 1 available and similarly, we use these digits to multiply powers of 2. For example:

2 becomes 10 which equals $1 \times 2 + 0 \times 1$ $(1 \times 2^1 + 0 \times 2^0)$
5 becomes 101 which equals $1 \times 4 + 0 \times 2 + 1 \times 1$ $(1 \times 2^2 + 0 \times 2^1 + 1 \times 2^0)$

Bearing this in mind, let's write out the first few binary numbers and see if you can work out some more:

If	1	is	1
and	2	is	10
	3	is	11
	4	is	100
	5	is	101

what are 6,7, and 8?

Binary numbers are important because computers store numbers in this form. Each of the digits of a binary number can be stored in a simple on/off form and it is easy to create electronic circuitry to store and manipulate numbers in this form. We shall return to this theme in chapter 6 and we give methods of converting between decimal and binary in chapter 9.

Factorials

$$n! = n \cdot (n - 1)!$$

When a number is written with an exclamation mark after it e.g. 4! it is shorthand to mean that the number is multiplied by all successive whole numbers down to 1. For example 4! means 4 x 3 x 2 x 1 which equals 24.

6! is 6 x 5 x 4 x 3 x 2 x 1 which equals 720. We refer to '4 factorial' and '6 factorial' and so on. It is a convenient shorthand used in some areas of maths and statistics.

What are the following equivalent to?

3!
7!
8!

Can you show that 8! Is equal to the number of minutes in February?

Some numbers are equal to the sum of the factorials of their own digits, for example:

145 = 1! + 4! +5! Can you prove this by doing the arithmetic?

We sometimes need to refer to 0! This doesn't mean anything using the above definition, but we use the convenient definition that 0! = 1.

Which of the following numbers form the sum of their individual factorials?

2
100
40585

Factorials and Permutations

How many ways can you arrange a number of objects? For example, if I have a red box and a yellow box, I can arrange them as red, yellow or yellow, red.

If I add a blue box, then I can arrange them in the following 6 ways:

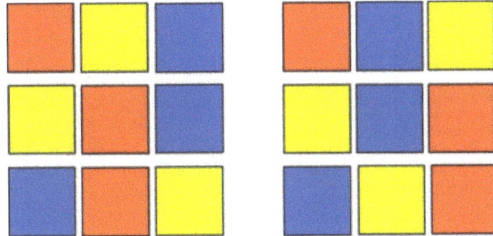

Question: if I now add a green box, how many ways can I arrange them? What do you notice about how many arrangements can be made for a given number of boxes? Without trying to write down all the possibilities, how many arrangements would there be if we went on to add a purple box?

Prime Numbers

Prime numbers have fascinated mathematicians for thousands of years and, surprisingly, have some practical uses in modern life.

A prime number is a positive whole number, greater than 1, that cannot be divided exactly by any other number than itself and 1. The first few primes are:

2, 3, 5, 7, 11, 13, 17 ......

There is no defined pattern to their occurrence and there are infinitely many of them (as proved by the famous ancient Greek mathematician, Euclid, in about 300 BC).

Which of the following numbers are prime?

14, 21, 23, 29, 33, 47, 73, 97

There is only one prime that is an even number, what is it? Some might say that makes it odd!

379009 is a prime number. If you enter this value into a calculator and turn it upside-down, what computer-related word do you find?

Prime numbers are an important part of security methods used for financial transactions over the internet.

Fibonacci Numbers

(Pronounced fib-on-archy)

This is a sequence of numbers that can be found in nature, such as in the sunflower head, but crops up in mathematics and has applications in computer science.

Given two starting numbers, successive numbers are generated by adding together the previous two numbers. We usually start with 1 and 1 to give:

   1, 1, 2, 3, 5, 8, 13 .....

What are the next six numbers in the sequence?

The sequence can begin with two other numbers, 0 and 1 are often chosen. Does this make a difference? What would the sequence become if we started with 1,3?

The Fibonacci Spiral

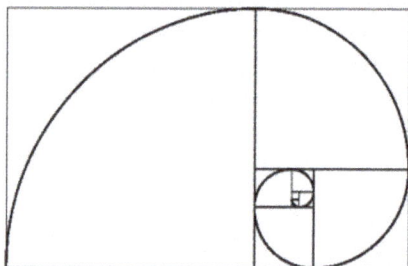

The Fibonacci sequence can be used to create a spiral that can be found in many natural occurrences such as shells, flowers and even spiral galaxies.

To construct a Fibonacci spiral, start off by drawing a small square, then use a pair of compasses to draw a radius that joins two corners, as shown:

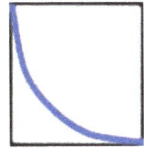

Next, draw another square of the same size to the right of the previous one and draw another radius that follows on from the one in the first square:

Now draw a bigger square above the two other squares with a side length equal to the length formed by the two squares. Use your compasses to draw a radius that follows on from the previous one:

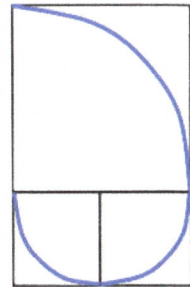

Now continue this process, drawing a bigger square to the left with a side length equal to the longest side of the large rectangle. Draw the radius as before.

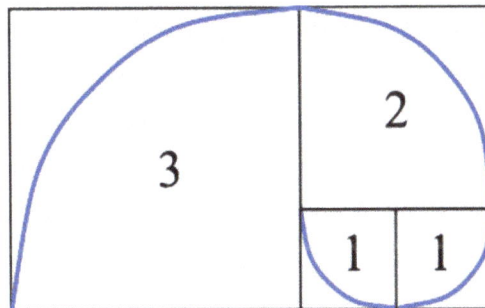

Keep on doing this until you have a spiral like the one shown at the start of this section. The Fibonacci sequence is used in computer science as a basis for searching and for certain storage structures. We shall return to it in chapter 4 when we discuss Pythagorean triples!

Congruent Numbers

Congruence is a useful concept in mathematics. In general terms it means a similarity, or agreement, between two things. For example, *congruent triangles* are ones that are identical – their sides are of the same length and the corresponding angles are the same.

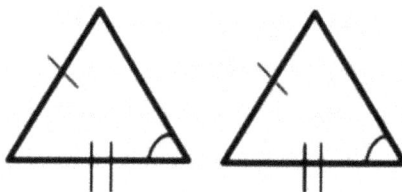

But what about *congruent numbers*?

Two numbers are said to be **congruent** if, when divided by a third number, they give the same remainder.

For example: 7 divided by 5 gives   1 remainder 2 (1 x 5 + 2)
                       12 divided by 5 gives   2 remainder 2 (2 x 5 + 2)

So 7 and 12 are congruent when divided by 5.

Which of the following pairs of numbers are congruent using the divisor given?

> 4 and 16 using divisor 3
> 6 and 8 using divisor 2
> 9 and 23 using divisor 7
> 2 and 5 using divisor 3
> 1 and 10 using divisor 3
> 1 and 100 using divisor 3
> 1 and 1000 using divisor 3
> 1 and 1,000,000 using divisor 3

Roman Numerals

We write numbers using *Arabic numerals* with the symbols 0,1,2,3,4,5,6,7,8,9 – so called because they were introduced to Europe by the Arabs in the 10th century. The history of numbers is quite interesting and evolved from making marks to help counting things and using different symbols for 1, 5, 10 and so on.

Roman numerals were an early way of representing numbers but are still used today in books for chapter numbers and for representing the year for certain TV and cinema productions. Roman numerals are often used on clocks and watches, although we often just read the time without thinking! You sometimes find clocks that use slightly incorrect Roman numerals e.g. IIII for 4 instead of IV. So what are the rules?

The numbers 1 to 10 in Roman numerals use the symbols I, V and X:

  I, II, III, IV, V, VI, VII, VIII, IX, X

Note that the numbers 4 and 9 make use of subtracting a single digit from the next value without any confusion! Also, we don't have any way of representing the number 0 (0 isn't one of the so-called *counting numbers* also called *natural numbers* but mathematicians argue about the latter!)

We also use L as 50, C as 100, D as 500 and M as 1000

From these, we can represent a range of numbers from 1 upwards e.g. 14 is XIV, 17 is XVII, 23 is XXIII, 39 is XXXIX, 72 is LXXII, 154 is CLIV, 359 is CCCLIX. Again, we can put a lower value before a bigger one to subtract it e.g. 95 would be XCV, but 99 would be XCIX and not IC. Hint: write your number as thousands, hundreds, tens and units before converting e.g. 99 is 90 + 9 giving XC + IX or XCIX. 594 = 500 + 90 + 4 giving D + XC + IV or DXCIV.
Now it's your turn! Work out the Roman numeral representation of the following numbers:

  11
  29
  47
  209
  1571
  2013
  1995

Can you draw a clock face which has all roman numbers from 1 to 12?
Imagine a digital watch that displays roman numerals!

And now convert the following numbers from Roman numerals to Arabic numerals:

    IX
    XVII
    CCXIV
    CXLIX
    MCMXLVI

Try doing the following arithmetical problems with Roman numerals – you'll soon see why they died out!

   a) VII + IV
   b) IX + XI
   c) XXI - IV

Whilst on this theme, have a look at the way the French use their numbers when talking. Although they write them in the same way as us (using Arabic numerals) they have an interesting way of constructing them verbally.

French Numerals in Speech

The numbers 0 to 16 have their own names 0 Zéro, 1 Un, 2 Deux, 3 Trois, 4 Quatre, 5 Cinq, 6 Six, 7 Sept, 8 Huit, 9, Neuf, 10 Dix, 11 Onze, 12 Douze, 13 Treize, 14 Quatorze, 15 Quinze, 16 Seize, but then you get:

    17 Dix-sept   (10+7)
    18 Dix-huit   (10+8)
    19 Dix-neuf   (10+9)

and   20 Vingt
          21 Vingt et un (20+1 uses *et* for *and*)
          22 Vingt-deux (20+2)

And continues this way up to 70 using trente (30), quarante (40), cinquante (50), soixante (60) when you get:

    70 Soixante-dix   (60+10)
    71 Soixante et onze (60+11)

72 Soixante-douze
73 Soixante-treize
74 Soixante-quatorze
75 Soixante-quinze
76 Soixante-seize
77 Soixante-dix-sept
78 Soixante-dix-huit
79 Soixante dix-neuf
80 Quatre-vingts   (4x20)
81 Quatre-vingt-un   (4x20 + 1 but doesn't use *et* as before)
82 Quatre-vingt-deux (4x20 + 2)
83 Quatre-vingt-trois (4x20 + 3)

So if thirty (30) is trente, 40 is quarante, and 50 is cinquante, what is the French for the following numbers:

32, 35, 41, 47, 52, 68

Try to find out about numbers in other languages e.g. German, Italian, Spanish and Greek.

Measurements of Time and Date

This is a whole topic by itself and perhaps we'll return to it later. For now, let's think about some things that relate to things we have already met.

Think of a clock (standard or digital) that displays the time in 12 hour format.

It goes from: 0 hours, 0 minutes, 1 seconds
to: 12 hours, 0 minutes, 0 seconds

Think about the seconds; they go from 0 to 59. In reality, they then go 60, 61, 62 etc. So we could say that the display shows *the remainder when then number of seconds is divided by 60.* Similarly, the minutes go from 0 to 59 so the display shows *the remainder when then number of minutes is divided by 60.*

We talked about remainders when we were looking at congruent numbers. We mathematicians have a special word for this: *modulo*.

So we say *63 modulo 60* is 3. In other words *63 divided by 60 leaves a remainder 3*.
This is usually written in a short form as (63 mod 60) = 3.
For our clock, we would have (actual seconds mod 60) = displayed number of seconds.

If 374 seconds have elapsed since midnight, the displayed number of seconds would be (374 mod 60) = 14.

Similarly for minutes. If 523 minutes had elapsed since midnight, the displayed number of minutes would be (523 mod 60) = 43

What about the hours? Let's assume we have a 12 hour display like analogue clocks and watches.

Try the following:

15 hours have elapsed since midnight what hour does the clock display?
How would we write this using modulo arithmetic?

87 hours have elapsed since midnight what hour does the clock display?
How would we write this using modulo arithmetic?

If we gave numbers to the days of the week, we could do the same. How would we number the days and what would be the modulo number (the divisor) in this case?
Using your result, show that the 3rd day of a month falls on the same day of the week as the 24th.

A useful trick with dates: Very often, we need to know the day of a given date in the month to come. For example, if today is 16th January and someone asks me *'what day of the week is the 25th February?'*, I can immediately respond with 'It is a Monday!'

How is this done? First I know that today is Wednesday. Now subtract the date from the number of days in the current month and add the new date. The result, modulo 7, is the number of days from the current day of the week.

In the above example, we know that today is Wednesday and that January has 31 days, so we get 31 − 16 + 25 = 40, 40 mod 7 = 5, and 5 days on from Wednesday gives you Monday. Alternatively, as we know that there are seven days in a week, we can count back two days instead of counting forward 5 days – easier if we are counting in the names of the day! So, in our example, two days back from Wednesday gives us Monday.

OK, it's not that amazing, but it often crops up in real life and impresses people when you can give the answer so quickly and certainly! It can be extended to more than one month in advance, by adding the number of days in each month – although the mental arithmetic becomes more tiresome!

Leap Years

Normally, years have 365 days, but every fourth year is declared a leap year with 366 days – the extra being added to the last day in February.

If the year is divisible by 4 then it is a leap year unless it is divisible by 100 except when it is divisible by 400.

If you were born on February 29th, in which of the following years would you not have a birthday?

    (i)   1984
    (ii)   2000
    (iii)   1992
    (iv)   2010
    (v)   2012

The above questions required us to know whether a number is divisible by 4. In chapter 1, we saw that a number is divisible by 4 if the last two digits (as a number) are divisible by 4. Alternatively, looking at just the last two digits, the number will be divisible by 4 if twice the tens-digit plus the ones digit is divisible by 4.

So, looking at the above:

1984: 2x8 + 4 = 20 which is divisible by 4, so 1984 is a leap year
2000: divisible by 400, so it is a leap year
1992: 2x9 + 2 = 20 which is divisible by 4, so 1992 is a leap year
2010: 2x1 + 0 = 2 which is not divisible by 4, so not a leap year
2012: 2x1 + 2 = 4 which is divisible by 4, so 2012 is a leap year

What about the following years?

2016
2022
1066
1984
2096

FURTHER QUESTIONS

1. Write 2 x 2 x 2 x 2 x 2 as a power of 2. What would this be in binary?

2. What is 9! ÷ 7! (Hint: save a bit of work by writing these out in full as a fraction)

3. 5 coins are laid out in a line on a table and 2 of these show 'heads', the rest are 'tails'. By listing all the possibilities, how many different arrangements of heads and tails can be achieved? Now calculate 5! ÷ (3! x (5 - 3)!) that is 5! ÷ (3! x 2!)

4. The pairs of primes that differ by 2 are called *twin prime pairs*. The first few are (3,5), (5,7), and (11,13). There are 5 more pairs before (101,103), can you find them?

5. What are the next 6 numbers in a Fibonacci sequence beginning with 3,5?

6. Which of the following pairs of numbers are congruent using the divisor given?

   4 and 7 using divisor 3, 4 and 21 using divisor 8, 15 and 22 using divisor 7.

7. What is 1254 in Roman Numerals?

8. What would be the French for: 27, 55, and 88?

9. A digital clock displays hours and minutes. If 2750 seconds have elapsed since midnght, what does the clock display?

10. The Battle of Waterloo was in the year 1815. Was this a leap year? When was the first leap year after this date?

Answers to Questions for Chapter Two

Binary Numbers

6 in binary is 110 (look at the binary numbers for 4 + 2)
7 in binary is 111
8 in binary is 1000

Factorials

3! = 3 x 2 x 1 = 6
7! = 7 x 6 x 5 x 4 x 3 x 2 x 1 = 5040
8! = 8 x 7! = 8 x 5040 = 40320

February has 28 days. Each day has 24 hours and each hour has 60 minutes, so the total number of minutes in February is 28 x 24 x 60 = 40320 which is equal to 8!

Note that 28 x 24 x 60 is (4 x 7) x (8 x 3) x (2 x 5 x 6) which can be re-arranged as:
        2 x 3 x 4 x 5 x 6 x 7 x 8

Numbers that are the sum of their individual factorials:

2 = 2!
100 does not equal 1! + 0! + 0! (1 + 1 + 1)
40565 = 4! + 0! + 5! + 8! + 5! = 24 + 1 + 120 + 40320 + 120

Factorials and Permutations

There are 24 ways of arranging the 4 boxes:

With 2 boxes, there are 2! arrangements
With 3 boxes, there are 3! arrangements
With 4 boxes, there are 4! arrangements

So, if there were 5 boxes, we would have 5! arrangements i.e. 120

Prime Numbers

Looking at the list:

14 is not prime because 14 = 2 x 7
21 is not prime because 21 = 3 x 7
23 is prime – no factors
29 is prime – no factors
33 is not prime because 33 = 3 x 11
47 is prime – no factors
73 is prime – no factors
97 is prime – no factors

The only prime number that is even is 2.

If you turn 379009 upside down on a calculator, you get GOOGLE the name of a well-known search engine! No doubt you can devise a trick to amaze your friends with this!

Fibonacci Numbers

Starting with 1, 1 we get 1, 1, 2, 3, 5, 8, 13, 21, 34, 55, 89, 144, 233, ...
If we start with 0, 1 we get 0, 1, 1 and the sequence continues as before.
If we start with 1,3 we get 1, 3, 4, 7, 11, 18, 29, 47, ...

Congruent Numbers

4 and 16 using divisor 3: 4 ÷ 3 = 1 remainder 1, 16 ÷ 3 = 5 remainder, 1 so congruent
6 and 8 using divisor 2: 6 ÷ 2 = 3 remainder 0, 8 ÷ 2 = 4 remainder 0, so congruent
9 and 23 using divisor 7: 9 ÷ 7 = 1 remainder 2, 23 ÷ 7 = 3 remainder 2, so congruent
2 and 5 using divisor 3: 2 ÷ 3 = 0 remainder 2, 5 ÷ 3 = 1 remainder 2, so congruent
1 and 10 using divisor 3: 1 ÷ 3 = 0 remainder 1, 10 ÷ 3 = 3 remainder 1, so congruent
1 and 100 using divisor 3: 1 ÷ 3 = 0 remainder 1, 100 ÷ 3 = 33 remainder 1, so congruent
1 and 1000 using divisor 3 : 1 ÷ 3 = 0 remainder 1, 1000 ÷ 3 = 333 remainder 1, so congruent
1 and 1,000,000 using divisor 3: 1 ÷ 3 = 0 remainder 1, 1,000,000 ÷ 3 = 333,333 remainder 1, so congruent

Roman Numerals

11 is represented as XI
29 is represented as XXIX
47 is represented as XLVII
209 is represented as CCIX
1571 is represented as MDLXXI
2013 is represented as MMXIII
1995 is represented as MCMXCV

A clock face which has all roman numbers from 1 to 12:

Roman numerals to Arabic numerals:

IX is 9
XVII is 17
CCXIV is 214
CXLIX is 149
MCMXLVI is 1946

Arithmetical problems with Roman numerals:

a) VII + IV is 7 + 4 = 11 which becomes XI
b) IX + XI is 9 + 11 = 20 which becomes XX
c) XXI − IV is 21 − 4 = 17 which becomes XVII

French Numerals

32 is trente-deux
35 is trente-cinq
41 is quarante et un
47 is quarante-sept
52 is cinquante-deux
68 is soixante-huit

Time and Date

15 hours after midnight would take us to 3pm the following day.
12 + 15 = 27 and (27 mod 12) = 3

87 hours after midnight would be 3 days and 15 hours later (3 x 24 + 15) or, again, 3pm
12 + 87 = 99 and (99 mod 12) = 3
We would number the days of the week from 0 to 6 and use 7 as the divisor e.g. if day 0
was a Sunday, day 9 would be (9 mod 7) = 2 i.e. Tuesday.

Assuming the days are numbered from 0 to 6, two dates in the month will fall on the
same day if the day number modulo 7 is the same e.g. 3rd June (3 modulo 7) = 3 and 24th
June (24 modulo 7) = 3, but note that day 0 corresponds to the day of the first of the
month.

Leap Years
2016 is a leap year
2022 is not a leap year
1066 is not a leap year
1984 is a leap year
2096 is a leap year

Answers to Further Questions

1. Write 2 x 2 x 2 x 2 x 2 = 2^5. In binary, this is 100000

2. 9! ÷ 7! = (9 x 8 x 7 x 6 x 5 x 4 x 3 x 2 x 1)/(7 x 6 x 5 x 4 x 3 x 2 x 1) = 9 x 8 = 72

3. There are 10 possible arrangements:

   HHTTT, HTTTH, TTTHH, HTHTT. HTTHT, THHTT, THTHT, THTTH, TTHHT, TTHTH

   5! ÷ (3! x 2!) = 120/12 = 10. The problem is an example of a *combination* and the number
   of arrangements can be calculated using factorials.

4. The next 5 twin prime pairs are: (17,19), (29,31), (41,43), (59,61), and (71,73)

5. The next 6 numbers are: 8, 13, 21, 34, 55, 89

6. Congruent: 4 and 7 using divisor 3, and 15 and 22 using divisor 7.

7. 1254 in Roman Numerals is MCCLIV

8. In French: 27 is vingt-sept, 55 is cinquante-cinq, and 88 is quatre-vingt–huit.

9. 2750/360 = 7 remainder 230, 230/60 = 3 remainder 50, so hours = 7, mins = 3

10. 1815 is an odd number, so not a leap year. the first leap year after this was 1816.

Chapter 3 Codes and Ciphers

Secret codes have been used for thousands of years – ancient Egyptians used hieroglyphs from before 3000 BC - an early example of coding even though these were not particularly secretive. They developed into different forms over the years, but essentially used pictures to represent ideas, sounds, or meanings.

Codes don't have to be for obscurity – they are commonly used as a short or convenient way to convey information. Computers use codes to represent letters and numbers. They also use codes to send information securely over the internet. We make extensive use of codes for postal addresses, telephone areas, shopping etc. However, we are probably most intrigued by the sort of codes that are used to send secret messages and we will look at these in some detail later.

Are codes and ciphers the same? Yes and no! A cipher (alternatively 'cypher') usually refers to the 'encryption' of some text in such a way so that outsiders cannot read it. A code can be the same thing but it can also refer to some known form of classification of information where it is easier or more convenient to represent the details in another form. We all use hand, eye, facial, and body signals to communicate – these form a sort of code that is understood by others. Dogs and cats have their codes to tell us some basic information – can you think of some examples?

Let's start by looking at some of the common codes we meet in everyday life.

Bar Codes

Bar Codes made their first appearance in the 1960s where early versions were used to identify railroad cars in the US, but it took nearly twenty years for them to be widely adopted. We recognise a typical barcode as an oblong strip containing alternate black and white lines of varying width as shown.

ISBN 978-1-908837-00-4

9 781908 837004

There are over 30 variations of this type of barcode used in different areas such as libraries, retail, industry, pharmacy and so on. Barcodes are often read by using a light and a photo sensor. Mobile phone users can download apps for reading barcodes with their phones.

The above bar code also contains another code - an ISBN Code - this is a 13 digit number that uniquely identifies a book (the International Standard Book Number). The digits represent various pieces of information including country, publisher and title.

In recent years, new scanning codes have appeared for use with mobile devices such as telephones. These codes are known as matrix codes and are a two dimensional form of bar code capable of holding more information in a given area. There are many varieties of these codes, a typical one is shown:

Morse Code

The Morse Code is well known for its use in radio communications. Samuel Morse and two other Americans developed an electric telegraph system in 1836. This system was designed to send a series of electrical pulses representing numbers and a code was used to represent individual numbers. This early Morse Code was extended to include letters and became the International Morse Code using dots and dashes (spoken as *dits* and *dahs)* for the short and long pulses.

A	● ▬		U	● ● ▬
B	▬ ● ● ●		V	● ● ● ▬
C	▬ ● ▬ ●		W	● ▬ ▬
D	▬ ● ●		X	▬ ● ● ▬
E	●		Y	▬ ● ▬ ▬
F	● ● ▬ ●		Z	▬ ▬ ● ●
G	▬ ▬ ●			
H	● ● ● ●			
I	● ●			
J	● ▬ ▬ ▬			
K	▬ ● ▬		1	● ▬ ▬ ▬ ▬
L	● ▬ ● ●		2	● ● ▬ ▬ ▬
M	▬ ▬		3	● ● ● ▬ ▬
N	▬ ●		4	● ● ● ● ▬
O	▬ ▬ ▬		5	● ● ● ● ●
P	● ▬ ▬ ●		6	▬ ● ● ● ●
Q	▬ ▬ ● ▬		7	▬ ▬ ● ● ●
R	● ▬ ●		8	▬ ▬ ▬ ● ●
S	● ● ●		9	▬ ▬ ▬ ▬ ●
T	▬		0	▬ ▬ ▬ ▬ ▬

Morse Code is still used today and is perhaps best known through the international distress signal SOS (dot dot dot dash dash dash dot dot dot) or through those beeps on some mobile phones when you get a text message (dot dot dot dash dash dot dot dot) - SMS - Short Message Service.

Question:

▪ — —   ▪▪▪▪   ▪ —   — / ▪▪   ▪▪▪ / ▪   ▪▪   — — ▪   ▪▪▪▪   — / — —   ▪▪   — ▪
▪▪ —   ▪▪▪ / ▪▪ — ▪   ▪▪   ▪▪▪ —   ▪ /

— — ▪   ▪▪   ▪▪▪ —   ▪ / — ▪ — —   — — —   ▪▪ —   ▪ — ▪ / ▪ —   — ▪   ▪▪▪
▪ — —   ▪   ▪ — ▪ / ▪▪   — ▪ / — ▪ — ▪   — — —   — ▪▪   ▪ / ▪ —   ▪▪▪ / ▪ — /
▪ — —   — — —   ▪ — ▪   — ▪▪ / ▪ —   — ▪   — ▪▪ / ▪ — / — ▪   ▪▪ —   — —   ▪   ▪
— ▪   ▪ —   ▪ — ▪▪ /

Semaphore

Semaphore is another type of code that has been used since the 19th century to send information by flags. In this system, two flags are moved to various positions to indicate different letters or numbers.

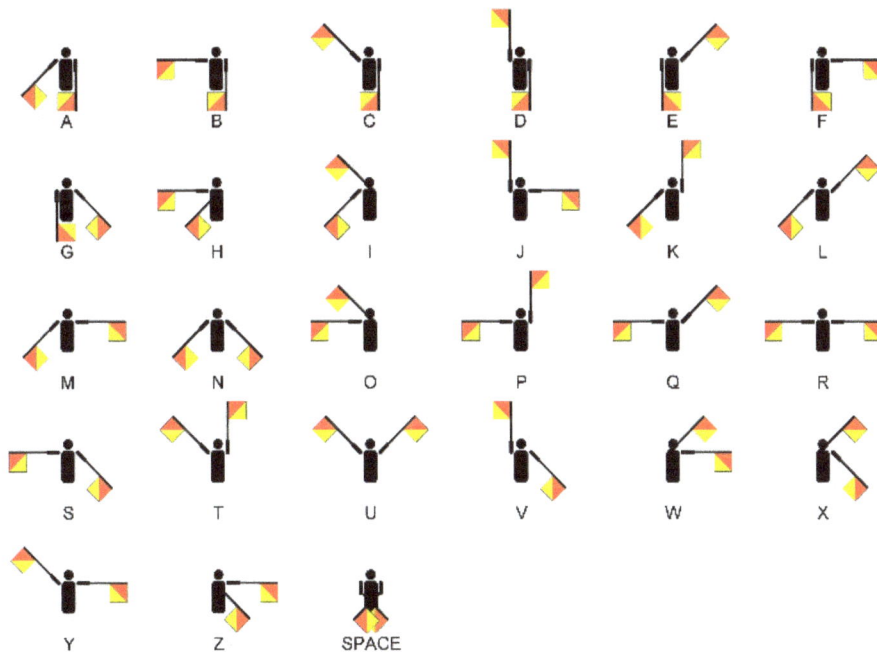

(Image courtesy of Wikimedia Commons)

33

These are shown from the view of someone facing the signaller. The letters A-K are also used for the digits 1 - 9 and 0. The signaller indicates that numeric values are to follow with the following signal:

To change back to letters, you use the J signal.
The flags shown above are the colours used at sea. On land we use blue and white flags.
What word is represented below?

Sign Language for the Deaf

BSL Fingerspelling Alphabet

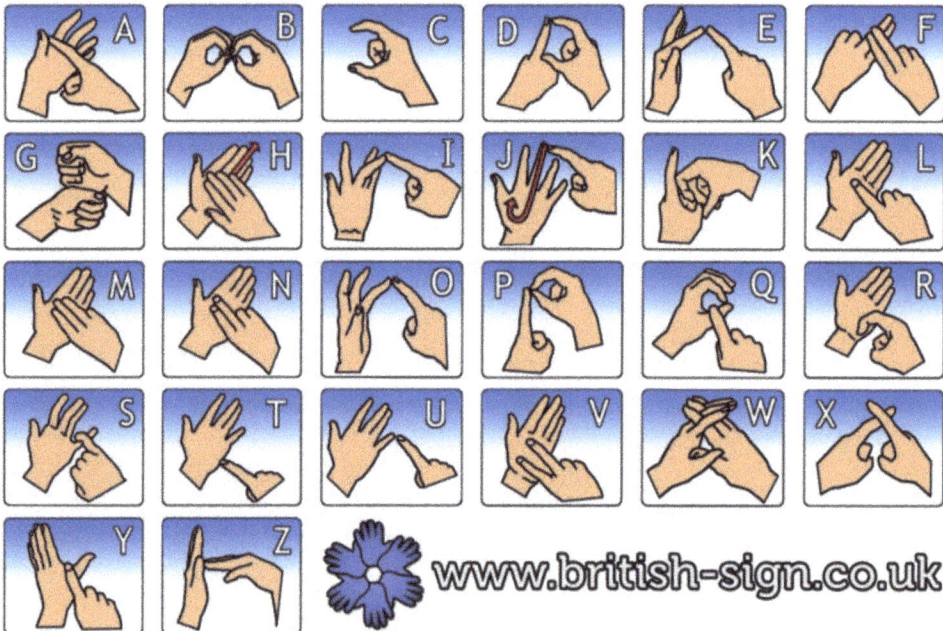

A B C D E F
G H I J K L
M N O P Q R
S T U V W X
Y Z

www.british-sign.co.uk

34

The pictures show how finger positions can be used to spell out particular letters of the alphabet. This is only part of the sign language and it would not be very convenient if we had to spell out every word in this way. Words and phrases typically involve movements of the hands and arms in a mime-like way. Examples can be found at britishsignlanguage.com. Note that other countries have their own sign languages that are sometimes quite different to British sign language.

Using the table above, try to translate the following:

Created on www.british-sign.co.uk

Created on www.british-sign.co.uk

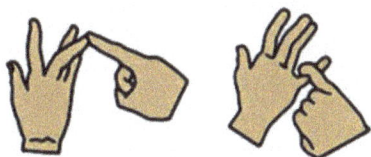

Created on www.british-sign.co.uk

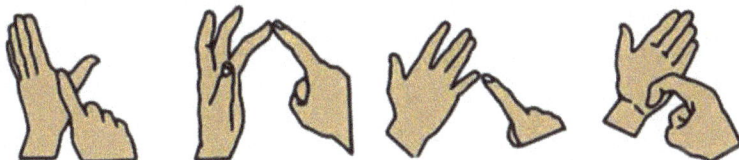

Created on www.british-sign.co.uk

Created on www.british-sign.co.uk

ASCII Code

The ASCII Code (American Standard Code for Information Interchange) was developed in the 1960s as a means of representing alphabetic and other characters in computers and communications equipment. The original code represented 128 characters and was widely used until 2007 when the UTF-8 code became more useful because it could represent a much wider range of characters.

The upper case letters A - Z are represented by the numbers 65 - 90
The lower case letters a - z are represented by the numbers 97 - 122
The digits 0 - 9 are represented by the numbers 48 - 57
Other characters such as space, +, -, ? are represented as 32, 43, 45, 63 respectively.

Try this:

87,72,65,84,32,73,83,32,49,50,32,43,32,49,57,63

Secret Codes

If you want to send a message to someone without anybody else being able to read it, you would need to disguise your message in some way. One possible method is to hide the message e.g. by writing it on a piece of paper using invisible ink. You can easily make invisible ink with lemon juice - put some in a bowl and use a thin stick to write your message with the 'ink' on a piece of paper. When it dries, the message should be invisible. To reveal it, heat the paper using a light bulb or hot radiator - taking care not to burn yourself or set the paper alight! Methods of hiding information like this are called *steganography*.

A commonly used method of coding is that of *substitution* whereby the letters of the alphabet are substituted for other letters or symbols. The simplest of these involves a simple shift of the letters as in the example below:

A	B	C	D	E	F	G	H	I	J	K	L	M	N	O	P	Q	R	S	T	U	V	W	X	Y	Z
G	H	I	J	K	L	M	N	O	P	Q	R	S	T	U	V	W	X	Y	Z	A	B	C	D	E	F

If we wanted to encode the word 'HELLO', we take each letter in turn, find it in the top row and read off the corresponding letter in the bottom row. So 'HELLO' becomes 'NKRRU'.

Here's a message encoded in the above cipher. Can you decode it?

O ZNOTQ ZNGZ EUA IGT XKGJ ZNOY!

A slight variation on this theme is to use a word or words with no repeated letters as a key and then list the remaining letters of the alphabet in order, starting with the letter following the last letter of the key word. For example, if the key was 'CAMERON' then the cipher would be:

A	B	C	D	E	F	G	H	I	J	K	L	M	N	O	P	Q	R	S	T	U	V	W	X	Y	Z
C	A	M	E	R	O	N	P	Q	S	T	U	V	W	X	Y	Z	B	D	F	G	H	I	J	K	L

Question: If, instead of starting the remaining letters with the next letter following the last one in the key word, we had started from the beginning of the alphabet, what problem would we meet? For example, in the above, we would follow CAMERON with BDFGH.......

Finding key words without repeated letters can be inconvenient so if we choose something like BOURTON ON THE HILL, we would simply miss out repetitions and use BOURTNHEIL, giving:

A	B	C	D	E	F	G	H	I	J	K	L	M	N	O	P	Q	R	S	T	U	V	W	X	Y	Z
B	O	U	R	T	N	H	E	I	L	M	P	Q	S	V	W	X	Y	Z	A	C	D	F	G	J	K

Question: What would be the problem if we used the same technique with the key words CHIPPING CAMPDEN?

Before we move on, let's return to the simple shift cipher for a moment. Remember our example:

A	B	C	D	E	F	G	H	I	J	K	L	M	N	O	P	Q	R	S	T	U	V	W	X	Y	Z
G	H	I	J	K	L	M	N	O	P	Q	R	S	T	U	V	W	X	Y	Z	A	B	C	D	E	F

We moved each letter along by 6 places, so that A became G, B became H and so on. When we got to encoding U, we went back to the start of the alphabet. If we cut out the table above and formed a ring by joining the ends, the alphabets in the rows would be continuous and our rule of 'move each letter forwards by 6 places' would describe the cipher completely.

Now suppose we are doing this on a computer. Each of the letters in our message to be encoded would be stored using its ASCII code. The table below gives the ASCII codes for upper case letters:

A	B	C	D	E	F	G	H	I	J	K	L	M	N	O	P	Q	R	S	T	U	V	W	X	Y	Z
65	66	67	68	69	70	71	72	73	74	75	76	77	78	79	80	81	82	83	84	85	86	87	88	89	90

So the word 'ADDITION' would become the sequence of numbers: 65, 68, 68, 73, 84, 73, 79, 78.

If we encoded 'ADDITION' with our simple shift cipher, the letters would become 'GJJOZOUT', for which the ASCII codes would be: 71, 74, 74, 79, 90, 79, 85, 84. As we would expect, the encoding has added 6 to each of the original ASCII codes.

But suppose we wanted to encode the word 'AUCTION', which becomes 'GAIZOUT' with corresponding ASCII sequences 65, 85, 67, 84, 73, 79, 78 and 71, 65, 73, 90, 79, 85, 84. So the rule doesn't work with the letter U (and wouldn't work for V,W,X,Y,Z). How can we write our rule to allow for the wraparound? Let's try:

'Add 6 to the ASCII code. If the result is bigger than 90, then subtract 26.'

Does this work? Try the letter U with ASCII code 85. If we add 6 to 85, we get 91. As 91 is bigger than 90, we subtract 26 to get 65 which is correct! But could we write our rule in a shorter form?

Cast your mind back to modulo arithmetic! Recall that a number modulo 26, gives the remainder when divided by 26. We shall use this although we need to do a bit of extra work!

If our letters A to Z had corresponding numbers 0 to 25, then we could simply use modulo 26 on any coded number to cope with the wraparound. For example X would be 23 which when coded with our shift of 6, would become 29. So if we took 29 modulo 26, we get 3 - which is the code for D - which is correct.

To achieve this, we take the ASCII code of a letter to be encoded and subtract 65, this gives us a number in the range 0 to 25 as required. We can then code the letter by adding 6 and use modulo 26. Finally, add 65 to get it back to a proper ASCII code.

So our new rule could be written as:

New ASCII Code = {(Old ASCII Code - 65 + 6)} modulo 26 + 65

That's neat, isn't it? What's more, we can translate that into computer program code almost directly. Here's a section of Python code that takes several letters in turn', codes them, and prints it new letter with its ASCII code:

```
for char in ["A","B","C","T","U","V","W","X","Y","Z"]:
    num = ord(char) # store its ASCII code in num
    codednum = ((num - 65) + 6)%26 + 65 # code it by adding 6 and ad-
justing
    print(codednum, chr(codednum))
```

Returning to substitution ciphers, there are a couple of historical examples that are worth mention.

The first example is the cipher used by Mary Queen of Scots during the later years of her imprisonment by her cousin, Queen Elizabeth I. In this cipher, symbols are substituted for characters and other symbols are used for commonly occurring words. The cipher is shown below.

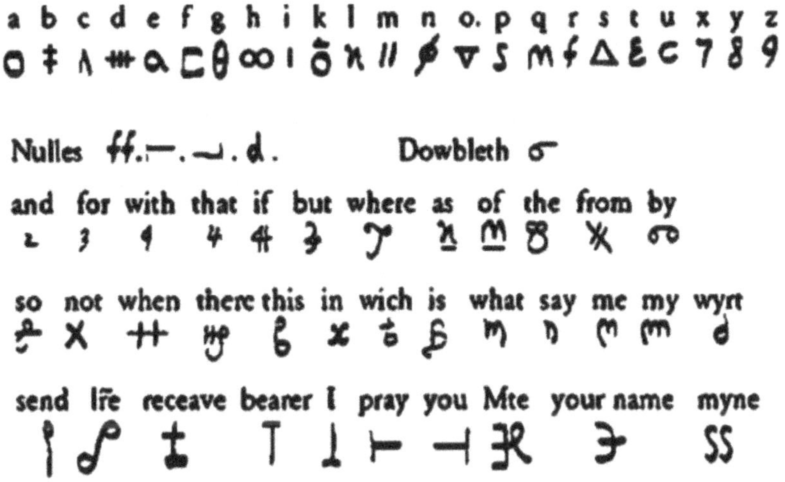

Messages were exchanged between Mary and a group of conspirators who intended to rescue her and overthrow Queen Elizabeth. Unfortunately for Mary, the messages were intercepted and deciphered, leading to the execution of the conspirators in 1586 and Mary in 1587.

The other example is 'The Adventure of the Dancing Men' set in 1898 which is one of the Sherlock Holmes stories by Sir Arthur Conan Doyle. At Ridling Thorpe Manor in Norfolk, strange drawings appear featuring matchstick figures of dancing men. An example is shown below:

Sherlock Holmes analyses the diagrams and cracks the code. The last picture that he deciphers reveals a sinister message! It is interesting to compare this cipher to the semaphore code described earlier.

The method used by Sherlock Holmes was that of *frequency analysis*. By this, we mean that for each letter in the coded message, we make a note of how many times it occurs and compare our results to a table of the occurrence of normal letters in a typical piece of text. This is the weakness of the substitution ciphers that we have looked at and, given a message of any significant length, frequency analysis will usually provide a means to decipher the code - particularly when it is a simple shift cipher!

An Italian man by the name of Alberti (1404-1472) suggested a more secure cipher using two, or more, substitute alphabets. As a simple example, we might use:

A	B	C	D	E	F	G	H	I	J	K	L	M	N	O	P	Q	R	S	T	U	V	W	X	Y	Z
H	I	J	K	L	M	N	O	P	Q	R	S	T	U	V	W	X	Y	Z	A	B	C	D	E	F	G
T	U	V	W	X	Y	Z	A	B	C	D	E	F	G	H	I	J	K	L	M	N	O	P	Q	R	S

Then we encode our message using the first alphabet (H,I,J,K...) for the first letter and the second alphabet (T,U,V,W ...) for the second letter and then back to the first alphabet for the third letter and so on.

So, for example the word 'DICTIONARY' becomes 'KBJMPHUTYR'. We see that the repeated letter I has been encoded differently into P and B, making frequency analysis more difficult. Decoding the message is a bit fiddly.

Can you decipher the message 'HEIXYMPL MBYLA GHFL PHL SXVG'?

Alberti's cipher was later developed further by Blaise de Vigenère and published in 1586. The Vigenère cipher was considered to be 'the uncrackable cipher' until around 1854 when Charles Babbage (designer of the first mechanical computer) devised a method of *cryptanalysis* that would break the code.

We have seen that codes use a key which is used by the sender to encipher a message and by the recipient to decipher it. A serious weakness of this system is that, at some stage the key itself has to be exchanged between sender and recipient. If this exchange is intercepted then the key is known by someone else who might also intercept any coded messages that follow. Also, the interceptor might change the message - as happened with Mary Queen of Scots when Sir Francis Walsingham (Queen Elizabeth's principal secretary and spymaster) arranged for her message to Anthony Babington to be altered so that he would reveal the names of his fellow conspirators.

An interesting solution to this is *public key cryptography* which is widely used today (including the encryption of personal data when you buy goods over the internet). The story is nearly always told using the people Alice and Bob who want to exchange a secret message and Eve, who is trying to eavesdrop on the secret conversation.

The mathematical theory behind this technique was introduced in 1977 by an American, Ronald Rivest who, along with his co-workers Adi Shamir and Leonard Adleman established the RSA cipher which works as follows:

Alice creates a key which is actually a pair of keys: a *public key* and a *private key*. She sends the public key to all her friends so that they can send secret messages to her. Bob wants to send a message to Alice, so he encrypts the message using Alice's public key and sends it to Alice. Now, Alice can decrypt the message with her private key because it is linked to her public key in a way that no-one knows. Eve, who has intercepted the message and also has Alice's public key cannot decrypt the message because it can only be read with Alice's private key and Alice doesn't share that with anyone! Not even Bob, who encrypted the message can decrypt it. If Alice wants to send a secret message back to Bob, she will need Bob's public key to encrypt it and it still doesn't matter if Eve has Bob's public key and she intercepts the message!

So, with modern cryptography each person generates a pair of keys - a public key and a private key. They freely distribute their public key which other people use to send encrypted messages to them. Nobody can decrypt a message with a public key. Only the owner of the private key can decrypt the messages.

Isn't that clever? The mathematics behind it is quite complicated, but it involves modular arithmetic and prime numbers. Who says that pure mathematics isn't useful!

When it comes to such things as sales over the internet and you are asked to send your credit card details, this method is used although you will be unaware that the seller has sent you their public key and that when you clicked the 'confirm sale' button, your details have been encrypted with their public key and sent back to them as a coded message.

But, that's all about secret codes for now. There are many other codes that can be found in everyday life. These include: Shorthand, Musical Notation, Post Codes, Telephone Codes, Colour Codes for Resistors, Computer Machine Codes and Computer Numerical Control (CNC) G-Codes for manufacturing. Can you find any others?

Let's just take a final look at another coding system that is in everyday use:

Check Digits

Suppose that you are selling something and I phone you up and ask to buy it using my credit card. I tell you my credit card number is **4829 4611 3807 2532** and after a moment, you say "Sorry, but that isn't a valid card number!" I check and find that I have accidentally switched two digits around and the card number should have been **4829 4611 8307 2532**. How did you know that my number was wrong?

The answer is that you did a calculation with the first 15 digits which resulted in a single digit 8 and as this did not match the actual last digit, 2, you knew that I had given you a wrong number! So how do we do that calculation?

Starting from the right hand side, ignore the rightmost digit and highlight each alternate digit from right to left.

4 8<mark>2</mark>9 4<mark>6</mark>1 1<mark>3</mark>8 0<mark>7</mark>2 5<mark>3</mark>

For each of the highlighted digits, double it and if the result is bigger than 9, subtract 9. Replace each highlighted digit with the corresponding result:

8 8<mark>4</mark>9 8<mark>6</mark>1 2<mark>6</mark>8 0<mark>7</mark>4 5<mark>6</mark>

Now add up all the digits: 8 + 8 + 4 + 9 + 8 + 6 + 2 + 1 + 6 + 8 + 0 + 7 + 4 + 5 + 6 = 82

Finally, take the last digit of your result and (if it is not 0) subtract it from 10 i.e. 10 - 2 = 8

So your check digit is 8 and as this does not match the last digit, 2, the number is not valid.

Let's try this again with the correct number:

4 8 2 9 4 6 1 1 8 3 0 7 2 5 3
8 8 4 9 8 6 2 1 7 3 0 7 4 5 6   (note 8 x 2 = 16, 16 - 9 = 7)

Now add up all the digits: 8 + 8 + 4 + 9 + 8 + 6 + 2 + 1 + 7 + 3 + 0 + 7 + 4 + 5 + 6 = 78

And the check digit is 10 - 8 = 2 and this corresponds to the last digit in the card number.

This method is used on all credit and debit cards. It is called the Luhn algorithm and is said to capture 98% of errors like the above. It doesn't detect an error if 90 gets replaced by 09 or vice versa.

That's all for now on this topic. Here's a few exercises based upon what we have covered in this chapter.

FURTHER QUESTIONS

1. Decode the following message:

▪ —   — ▪   — — —   —   ▪ ▪ ▪ ▪   ▪   ▪ — ▪ / —   — ▪ — —   ▪ — — ▪   ▪ /
— — —   ▪ ▪ — ▪ / — ▪ — ▪   — — —   — ▪ ▪   ▪ / ▪ ▪   ▪ ▪ ▪ /
— ▪ ▪ ▪   ▪ — ▪   ▪ —   ▪ ▪   ▪ — ▪ ▪   ▪ — ▪ ▪   ▪ /

2. Translate into Morse Code: SEMAPHORE WAS INVENTED BY CLAUDE CHAPPE

3. What message is conveyed by the following semaphore signals?

(Images courtesy of Wikimedia Commons)

4. The diagram below uses British sign language to spell the name of a famous mathematician. Who is it?

Created on www.british-sign.co.uk

5. Translate the following message into ASCII code:

    37 IS A PRIME NUMBER

6. Using the simple shift cipher in this chapter, what does the following message say?

    YKIXKZ IUJKY GXK AYKJ HE YVOKY

7. The message below was created with a different simple cipher (but the encoded letters still follow alphabetical order as before).

    O GSQFSH QCRS WG BSJSF HCHOZZM GSQIFS

   Use Sherlock Holmes' technique by counting how many times each letter appears in the message and finding the most frequent. Which letter of the alphabet do you think occurs most often? Can you use this to crack the cipher and decode the message?

8. In this chapter, we devised a secret code that added 6 to the ASCII code of each letter in a message and if the result was greater than 90, we subtracted 26. This rule only applies to upper case letters. Using this method, write the word 'MODULO' in code.

9. We found that another way of specifying the rule in question 8 is:
    New ASCII Code = {(Old ASCII Code - 65 + 6)} modulo 26 + 65
   We also know that the lower case letters a - z have ASCII codes 97 - 122 respectively. Why does this rule not work for lower case letters?

10. The following message has been encoded using the Alberti cipher as given earlier in this chapter:

    AAHM ZAHESHA

Answers to Questions for Chapter Three

Morse Code

The question reads:

WHAT IS EIGHT MINUS FIVE

GIVE YOUR ANSWER IN CODE AS A WORD AND A NUMERAL

So the answer is: THREE 3 which in Morse code is:

—   ••••   •—•   •   • / •••——

Semaphore

The word is HELLO

Sign Language

The message reads: HELLO WHAT IS YOUR NAME

ASCII Code

WHAT IS 12 + 19?

84,72,69,32,65,78,83,87,69,82,32,73,83,32,51,49

Secret Codes

The message reads: I THINK THAT YOU READ THIS!

The problem is that the final letters S to Z stay the same after coding!

CHIPNGAMDE: A similar problem occurs. The letters Q to Z stay the same after coding.

Alberti Cipher: ALBERTI'S FIRST NAME WAS LEON (apostrophe added after decoding)

1. ANOTHER TYPE OF CODE IS BRAILLE

2. ••• • —— •— •——• •••• ——— —•— •/ •—— •— •••
   /•• —• •••— • —• — • —••/—••• —•——/

   —•—• •—•• •— ••— —•• •/

   —•—• •••• •— •——• •——• •/

3. HIGH TIDE

4. GAUSS (Carl Friedrich Gauss 1777 - 1855)

5. 51, 55, 32, 73, 83, 32, 65, 32, 80, 82, 73, 77, 69, 32, 78, 85, 77, 66, 69, 82

6. SECRET CODES ARE USED BY SPIES

7. A SECRET CODE IS NEVER TOTALLY SECURE

8. 83, 85, 74, 65, 82, 85

9. The method doesn't work for lower case letters because we are subtracting 65 (the ASCII code for 'A') instead of 97 (the ASCII code for 'a').

   Consider using the rule for 'a':

   97 - 65 = 32, 32 + 6 = 38, 38 modulo 26= 12, 12 + 65 = 77 (outside original range)

   Instead, subtract 97. So for 'a':

   97 - 97 = 0, 0 + 6 = 6, 6 modulo 26 = 6, 6 + 97 = 103 (the code for 'g')

   And doing the same for 'z':

   122 - 97 = 25, 25 + 6 = 31, 31 modulo 26 = 5, 5 + 97 = 102 (the code for 'f')

10. THAT SHALLOT

Chapter 4   Square Roots, Imaginary Numbers, Triangles and More Fibonacci

The Common Theme - Squares!

We all know what a square is - a four sided shape with parallel sides of equal length and internal angles of 90 degrees.

The area of a square is, like a rectangle, is its length times its width - so, for a square, its area is its length times its length.

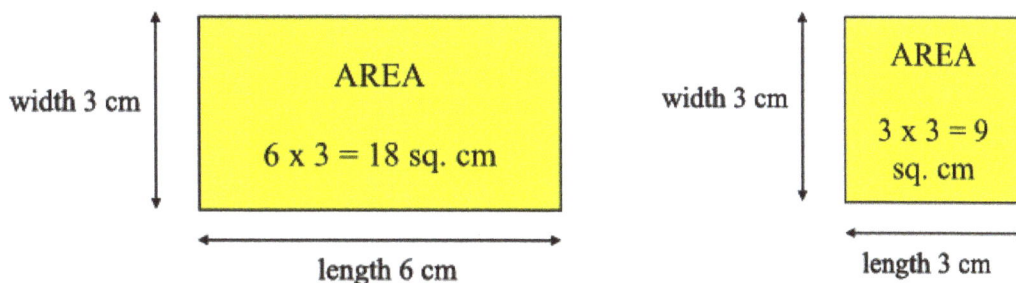

width 3 cm

AREA

6 x 3 = 18 sq. cm

length 6 cm

width 3 cm

AREA

3 x 3 = 9 sq. cm

length 3 cm

We talk about the square of a number as being the number multiplied by itself. For example the square of 5 is 5 x 5 = 25. We also refer to '5 squared' as the same thing although, in mathematics, this has a subtle reference to the more general idea of where numbers can be multiplied by themselves many times (called the power or index). When we want to write things like 'five squared' we write 5^2 (5 to the power 2, or 5 x 5 - the little raised number indicates how many times the number is multiplied by itself)

That leads us on to the idea of the **square root** of a number - which, if we think back to the square shape is the length of the side, given its area. For example, the square root of 9 is 3 because 3 x 3 = 9. Similarly, the square root of 4 is 2 and the square root of 16 is 4.

Not all square roots turn out to be whole numbers. For example, the square root of 6 is 2.45 (approximately). Fortunately, most calculators have a square root button with the symbol √. To work out the square root of a number by yourself can be a bit tricky but here's an interesting way of finding a square root by making a guess then using a simple calculation to get a better guess, then using the better guess to get an even better guess, and so on. It's a bit easier if you use a calculator, but can be done without.

The rule is:

- Make a guess at the square root of your original number
- Divide your original number by the guess
- Add the result to the guess
- Divide the new result by 2: this becomes the new guess
- Repeat the process until you have sufficient accuracy

For example, find the square root of 6.
First guess: 2
6/2 = 3
3 + 2 = 5
5/2 = 2.5

Next round:
First guess: 2.5
6/2.5 = 2.4
2.5 + 2.4 = 4.9
4.9/2 = 2.45 (as we said before)

This way of calculating the square root is often called "Newton's method" and is a particular example of a general technique for solving tricky equations devised by Sir Isaac Newton and first published in 1685. Interestingly, this method produced the same procedure as another way of finding square roots, known as the *Babylonian method* which is attributed to the ancient Greek mathematician and engineer, Hero of Alexandria, 10 - 70 AD. He was a very talented man who also invented the first vending machine and had the concept of an imaginary number - although such numbers were not to be 'discovered' until the 16th century!

Try this one! What is the square root of 14? Give your answer to 2 decimal places.

Imaginary Numbers

If you multiply two numbers, the rule in maths is that a 'positive times a positive' is a positive, 'a positive time a negative' is a negative, and a 'negative times a negative' is a positive. For example:

$$3 \times 4 = 12 \qquad -3 \times 4 = -12 \qquad 3 \times -4 = -12 \qquad -3 \times -4 = 12$$

This was fine until someone said "I've got an equation for a real problem and I need to find the square root of a negative number!" Well, the existing numbers couldn't supply the solution - but it was known that a solution did exist for this real problem. So they said "OK, let's say that the square root of -1 is an imaginary number called i" and this solved all the problems! We get $i^2 = -1$ and if we want the square root of -9 we just rewrite this as 9 x -1 and we get $\sqrt{-9} = \sqrt{9} \times \sqrt{-1} = 3i$ (a shorthand way of writing 3 x i).

So, think about multiplying a number by i several times. For example, start with 2 and multiply by i several times:

    2   2.i   2i.i   2i.i.i   2i.i.i.i and so on (where '.' indicates multiplication)

this is the same as:

    2   2i $2i^2$ $2i^3$ $2i^4$ and so on

So, if $i^2 = -1$ then we get:

    2   2i   -2   -2i   2   and so on

So how do we relate this to our normal numbers? One way is to consider how we think of our normal positive and negative numbers. We can think of these numbers as being on a line - like a ruler:

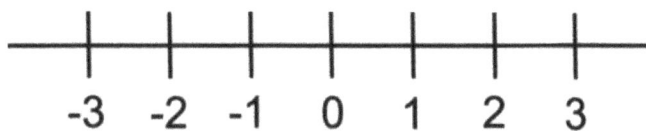

So where are the imaginary numbers? We think of these as being at right angles to the standard numbers, as shown overleaf:

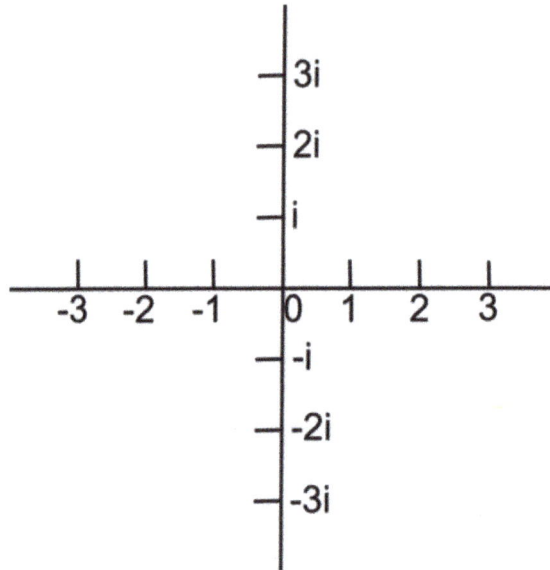

This is called an *Argand* Diagram - accredited to the French mathematician Jean-Robert Argand (1768–1822), but first described by Caspar Wessel (1745–1818).

We can see that if we multiply a number by i, it rotates anticlockwise by 90°. So if we start with +2 and multiply by i, we get i2. If we then multiply i2 by i, we get $i^2$2 and since i^2 equals -1, this equals -2. You can follow this through by multiplying by i until you get back to +2 on the real axis.

Looking at the Argand diagram, we can relate this to a normal graph or a map, where any point in the area of the chart can be identified by its *coordinates*. We specify any point by looking at its horizontal and vertical components - for example look at the point in the diagram below:

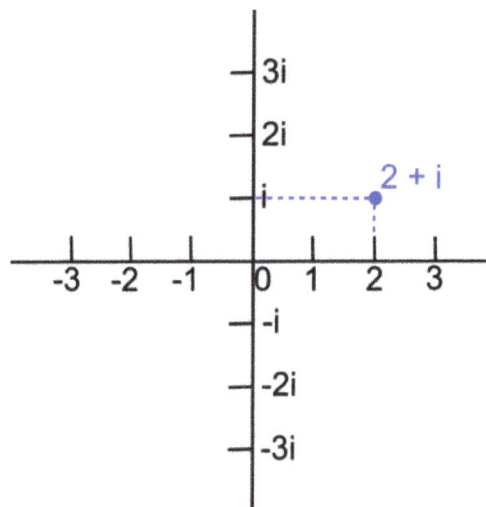

We see that the point shown is measured by 2 on the real axis and by 1 on the imaginary axis, so we call this number 2 + i. So, does it hold true that if we multiply this number by i, we move it through 90°? Let's work it out. Starting with (2 + i) and multiplying by i, we get (2 + i) x i which equals $2i + i^2 = 2i - 1$

Try drawing the point 2i -1 (which can be written as -1 + 2i) on a sheet of graph paper and see if that point has rotated through 90°. Hint: Draw an arrow from 0 (the *origin*) to the first point (2 + i) and rotate this anticlockwise through 90° (a quarter of a circle).

A number that has both real and imaginary components is called a **complex number**.

Pythagoras

The famous Greek mathematician, Pythagoras in around 500 BC, gave us a rule for working out the lengths of the sides of triangles that have one angle of 90°. The 90° angle is called a 'right-angle' and the side of the triangle opposite to this angle is called the 'hypotenuse'.

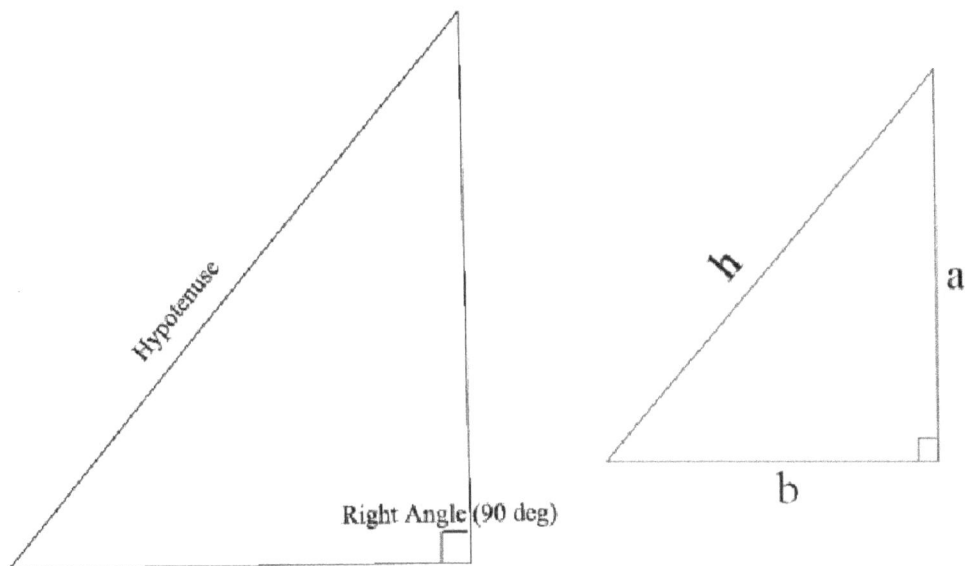

Pythagoras showed that the lengths of the sides were related by the squares of their lengths.

The shortest way of saying this is: $h^2 = a^2 + b^2$ or, as Pythagoras put it 'the square on the hypotenuse is equal to the sum of the squares on the other two sides'

So, for example, if we had the triangle shown below:

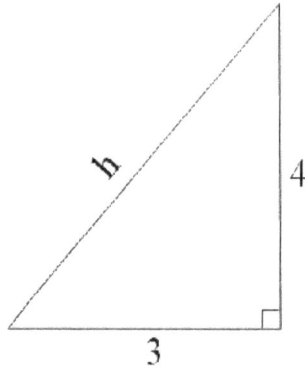

The (length of the hypotenuse) squared: h^2, would be $3^2 + 4^2$ which equals $9 + 16 = 25$
So the hypotenuse, h, would be $\sqrt{25}$ which is 5

Here's one for you (you might need a calculator!) - what is the length of the hypotenuse, h?

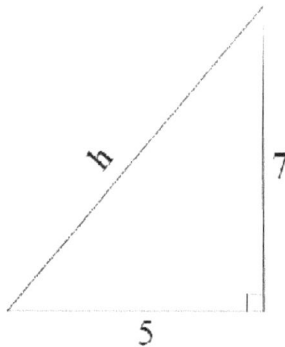

As you can see, most right-angled triangles don't have such a neat result as my first example where all the sides are whole numbers. The 3,4,5 triangle is the first, the next one is 5,12,13 and the next is 8,15,17. These special numbers are called **Pythagorean Triples**.

Although a right-angled triangle with sides 6,8,10 will still obey the rule ($6^2 + 8^2 = 36 + 64$ $=100 = 10^2$) it is not considered to be a true Pythagorean triple because the sides are simply double the lengths of the 3,4,5 triangle!

Now prepare yourself for a bit of magic! I'm going to show you how Pythagorean triples are related to the Fibonacci sequence!

Fibonacci

Do you remember our old friend, Fibonacci? His name is associated with the sequence 1,1,2,3,5,8,13,21 .... whereby we start with two numbers (usually 1 and 1) and generate following terms by adding the two previous numbers.

Now let's see the link between the Fibonacci sequence Pythagorean triples:

- Generate a Fibonacci sequence using 2 starting values e.g. 1,1,2,3,5,8,13,21......
- Write down any 4 consecutive Fibonacci numbers from the sequence e.g. 1,2,3,5
- Multiply the outer numbers: $1 \times 5 = 5$
- Multiply the inner numbers and double the result: $2 \times 3 = 6$, $2 \times 6 = 12$
- These two numbers (in our example 5 and 12) form two sides of a Pythagorean triple.
- $5^2 + 12^2 = 25 + 144 = 169$, so the hypotenuse is $\sqrt{169} = 13$

Try this: generate a Fibonacci sequence starting with 2 and 7 and then use the first 4 terms to generate a Pythagorean triple. What are the lengths of the sides? Is this a true Pythagorean triple? If not, what is the underlying triple? If so, could this other triple have been generated from a Fibonacci sequence?

There is another relationship between Fibonacci and Pythagorean triples. Generate the standard sequence beginning with 1, 1 to get 1, 1, 2, 3, 5, 8, 13, 21, 34, 55, 89, 144, 233, 377, ...

Now, start from the 5th term and highlight alternate terms:

1, 1, 2, 3, 5, 8, 13, 21, 34, 55, 89, 144, 233, 377, ...

The highlighted terms happen to be the lengths of the hypotenuses of Pythagorean triples. For example: $89^2 = 39^2 + 80^2$ - check this on your calculator!

Try this: given the hypotenuse lengths 5, 13, 34, what are the corresponding pair of sides in each case? You will probably have found that this is more tricky because you are given one number (the hypotenuse) and trying to find two other numbers whose squares add up to the first number. This gets more tricky as the numbers get bigger!

Primitive Pythagorean Triples

As we said earlier, we can devise Pythagorean triples by simply taking a known triple and multiplying each number by another positive whole number e.g. given that $5^2 + 12^2 = 13^2$ If we multiply the lengths by 2 we get $10^2 + 24^2 = 26^2$ (check this out on your calculator). But, because these are only simple scaled-up versions of the original triangles, we don't regard them as true Pythagorean triples. We distinguish the original triples by calling them *Primitive Pythagorean Triples,* so (3,4,5) is a primitive Pythagorean triple but (6,8,10) is not.

We have looked at how a Fibonacci sequence can be used to discover Pythagorean triples. There are various other methods dating back as far as around 300 BC to the Greek mathematician, Euclid - so this has been an interesting topic for quite a while!

Euclid's idea was that we take two positive whole numbers (let's call them M and N) and M is bigger than N. For example, let M and N be 5 and 3. One side of our triple will be $5^2 - 3^2 = 25 - 9 = 16$. Another side of the triple will be $2 \times (5 \times 3) = 30$ and the remaining side will be $5^2 + 3^2 = 25 + 9 = 34$. So, does $16^2 + 30^2 = 34^2$? You can check this on your calculator. Is this a primitive triple?

What do you get with the following values for M and N: 3,1 and 7,4

So, there we are - that simple square that we started off with has shown us some interesting and surprising results that intertwine. Would it surprise you to find that you can also use complex numbers to prove Euclid's formula?

I hope that you have enjoyed this little adventure into numbers and geometry. Just one last point, to make descriptions easier in future, we call the whole numbers (positive, negative and zero) ***integers***.

But we can't leave our chapter on squares without mentioning another type of square:

Magic Squares

You may have come across these before, these are square grids filled with the numbers 1,2,3,4 ... such that if you look at any row, column, or diagonal, the numbers add up to the same total. We shall consider grids with an odd number of rows and columns. Have a look at the 3x3 grid below:

8	1	6
3	5	7
4	9	2

Now you can create a magic square by trial and error, but it's hard work! So let's have a look at a method for such squares where they have an odd number of rows and columns. It will help to imagine that our square is written on a piece of paper that can be rolled round so that the right hand side joins the left hand side. Similarly, rolling it another way would result in the top being joined to the bottom. Got that? OK here we go then …

Start off by putting a 1 in the middle square of the top row.
Next, we are going to place the numbers 2 to 9 in turn, locating the next square by going diagonally upwards to the right:

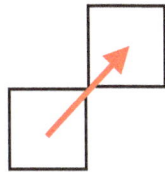

So 2 would go in the square above and to the right of 1 - but there isn't one! However, if the top of the grid is joined to the bottom, then we can place the number 2 in the 3rd column of the 3rd row, as seen on the previous page.

Similarly with 3, we go off the right-hand side and re-emerge at the left-hand side. So 3 goes in the first column of the second row.

Now, we try and place 4 using the same rule, but we hit a snag here - the square is already filled! So, we need one more rule: if the attempted square is already filled, we come back to where we were and drop down one square.

So 4 would go in the square where 1 is, so we drop down one square from 3 and put 4 in the first column of the third row.

Now carry on filling up the grid by following these rules.

Can you create a 5 x 5 magic square? What is the magic total?

Let's finish off the chapter with some further questions.

FURTHER QUESTIONS

1. Use Newton's method to find the square root of 42 correct to 2 decimal places. Start with an initial guess of 7.

2. What do we get if we multiply 3i by 7i ? (i being $\sqrt{-1}$)

3. What is (5 + 9i) - (4 + 6i) ?

4. Find the length of the hypotenuse of a right-angled triangle whose other sides have lengths of 4cm and 7cm.

5. A triangle has sides of length 5cm, 6cm and 8cm. Is it right-angled?

6. Use starting values of 1 and 3 to generate a Fibonacci sequence with 10 terms.

7. Use the second to the fourth terms of the sequence in question 6 to generate a Pythagorean triple. Is this a primitive triple?

8. Use the values 4 and 2 with Euclid's method to generate a Pythagorean triple.

9. Is the Pythagorean triple in question 8 a primitive triple?

10. Create a 7 x 7 magic square. What is the magic total?

Answers to Questions for Chapter Four

<u>Square Roots</u>

The square root of 14 is 3.74 (to 2 decimal places)

<u>Pythagoras</u>

The length of the hypotenuse is 8.6 (approximately)

<u>Fibonacci</u>

2, 7, 9, 16, ...

Multiply the outer numbers: 2 x 16 = 32

Multiply the inner numbers and double the result: 7 x 9 x 2 = 126

$32^2 + 126^2 = 1024 + 15876 = 16900 = 130^2$

Not a true Pythagorean triple, since the sides are double that of 16, 63, 65

and $16^2 + 63^2 = 65^2$

It can be shown that the side length created by the two inner terms is the larger of the two. Since this is twice the product of the two inner terms, the result must be an even number. As 63 is an odd number, it could not be generated from a Fibonacci sequence.

$3^2 + 4^2 = 5^2$

$5^2 + 12^2 = 13^2$

$16^2 + 30^2 = 34^2$

<u>Euclid</u>

M = 3, N = 1: $3^2 - 1^2 = 8$, 2 x 3 x 1 =6, $6^2 + 8^2 = 10^2$ (scaled 3,4,5 triple)

M = 7, N = 4: $7^2 - 4^2 = 49 - 16 = 44$, 2 x 7 x 4 = 56, $33^2 + 56^2 = 65^2$

Magic Squares

17	24	1	8	15
23	5	7	14	16
4	6	13	20	22
10	12	19	21	3
11	18	25	2	9

Magic Total = 65

Answers to Further Questions

1. $42/7 = 6$, $6 + 7 = 13$, $13/2 = 6.5$

    $42/6.5 = 6.462$, $6.462 + 6.5 = 12.962$, $12.962/2 = 6.481$

    The next step gives the same result, so $\sqrt{42} = 6.48$ to 2dp

2. -21 because $3i \times 7i = 21i^2$ and $i^2 = -1$

3. $(5 + 9i) - (4 + 6i) = 1 + 3i$

4. $4^2 + 7^2 = 16 + 49 = 65$, $\sqrt{65} = 8.06$, so hypotenuse = 8.06 cm

5. Not right-angled because $5^2 + 6^2$ is not equal to 8^2

6. 1, 3, 4, 7, 11, 18, 29, 47, 76, 123

7. $3 \times 11 = 33$, $2 \times 4 \times 7 = 56$, $33^2 + 56^2 = 4225 = 65^2$ (it is a primitive triple)

8. $4^2 - 2^2 = 12$, $2 \times 4 \times 2 = 16$, $12^2 + 16^2 = 20^2$ so the triple is (12, 16, 20)

9. Not a primitive triple because it is a scaled up (3, 4, 5) triple

10.

30	39	48	1	10	19	28
38	47	7	9	18	27	29
46	6	8	17	26	35	37
5	14	16	25	34	36	45
13	15	24	33	42	44	4
21	23	32	41	43	3	12
22	31	40	49	2	11	20

Magic Total = 175

Chapter 5   Misdirections, Philosophy, Paradoxes and Logic

Don't believe everything you are told! On the face of it, this piece of advice is a statement of the obvious and most of us make some form of check on what others tell us. This check usually takes the form of thinking of this new information in relation to what we already know. If it agrees with our existing knowledge and we respect the source of this new information, we are likely to accept it.

This chapter looks at ways in which we can be deceived by information - particularly numerical data. In this context, we introduce some common mathematical and statistical tricks and go on to consider logic and see how we can solve problems involving logic.

These are situations where we can be duped involving mathematics - very often involving percentages and statistics. You only have to listen to politicians (and others with some purpose) to reveal some rather strange claims. A great book that reveals many secrets is "How to Lie with Statistics", by Darrell Huff. This should be essential reading for anyone who enjoys revealing the inconsistencies in the information that the public is given!

But first, let us enjoy some great examples of apparent contradictions in everyday life. Consider the following scenario:

Three friends go to a restaurant for a meal together. After they have enjoyed a modest feast, the waiter brings the bill which shows a total of £30. The friends decide to split the cost between them and each put £10 on the plate which is then collected by the waiter.

However, when the waiter gets back to the till, he discovers an error in his original calculations and finds that they should have only been charged a total of £25. So he puts their £30 into the till and takes five £1 coins out. Being slightly dishonest and not very good at arithmetic he decides to give them back £1 each and puts the remaining two £1 coins into his pocket. The diners are happy because their meal was cheaper than they thought and the waiter is happy because he has £2 in his pocket. Also the restaurant's manager is happy because the contents of the till are correct. All very good! But, if the three diners each paid £9, that's a total of £27 and there is £2 in the waiter's pocket, giving a grand total of £29. But they gave the waiter £30, so what happened to the other pound?

Any budding mathematician is always on the alert for dodgy information given in the media. Some of it is accidental, while other information is conveniently manipulated. The most common misdirections are reports that don't specify the essential information. Take, for example, a politician that claims we are spending 50 million pounds on [project X]. Unfortunately, this doesn't include the timescale - is it over 1 year, 5 years, 10 years? Also, such statements have been known to be presented as new announcements when, in fact, the figures incorporate money that was announced a year or so before for the same project.

The other figures that are most common to abuse are percentages and averages. Let's have a look at these in turn, with some examples of how things can be twisted to reinforce a point of view.

Misdirections

Dubious Percentages

In order to appreciate how people can put some falsehoods by us, we must make sure that we are clear on the basic facts. Let's just remind ourselves of the basics. The percentage of a number is obtained by multiply the number by the 'percentage' and dividing by 100. For example 5% of 60 is (5 x 60)/100 = 300/100 = 3. The term 'percent' refers to 'parts per hundred'.

We talk about percentage increases and decreases, so how are these calculated? There are two basic calculations here. First consider a 5% increase. This means that we end up with 105% of the original (100% + 5%). For example, if I lend Jack £80 for a year with an interest rate of 5%, then he must pay me back 80 x 105/100 = £84. For percentage decreases, we deduct the percentage from 100%. For example, if I buy a car for £6,000 and its value depreciates by 5% per year then in one year's time it will be worth 6000 x 95/100 = £5,700.

But we must be clear about what the percentage is of - and here lies a source of confusion!

For example, a baker says that all her costs have risen by 12% so she puts all her prices up by 12%, But, a week later she says that she has decided to absorb the increases herself and reduces all the prices by 12% - so are we now paying the same as we did before the increase? If I used to pay £2.50 for a cake before the increase, what do I now pay?

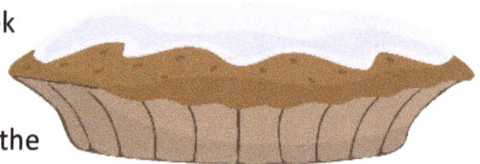

Averages

We all think that we know what is meant by the word 'average' and this is why some people use it to deceive us with genuine figures. They can get away with this because there are different averages: the mean, median and mode - each usually give a different figure, so a very convenient device if you want to mislead or persuade someone!

The 'mean' is what most people understand by 'average' (add the values and divide the total by the number of items), whereas the median is the midway value and the mode is the most commonly occurring. Each of these has its place when describing data but, sadly, the method is often selected to suit the argument!

Here's an example. A small company has 5 employees who each earn £300 per week and the boss pays himself £1000 per week. The mean weekly wage is £2500/6 = £416.67 but this is considerably more than the wage paid to each employee!

<u>*Philosophy*</u>

Sometimes we get a similar situation that we might describe as a philosophical problem where we have to analyse our meaning and understanding to resolve an issue. An example is the case of the hunter and the bear. Consider the following: 'One day a hunter enters a forest and sees a bear climbing a tree. Being a hunter, he tries to shoot the bear, but the bear is clever and, upon seeing the hunter, moves around the tree so that the tree is between him and the hunter. The hunter spots the evasive action of the bear and moves steadily clockwise around the tree in pursuit of the bear. The cunning bear is aware of the hunter's intent and also moves around the tree in such a way that the tree is always between him and the hunter.' The question is: Does the hunter go around the bear?

<u>*Paradoxes*</u>

Now let's have a look at another situation where we arrive at an apparent contradiction involving statements about possible scenarios. One of the classic paradoxes goes along the following lines:

'The people from the land of Fibonia are called Fibonians and they are all liars.
Everything they say is a lie. Even a Fibonian will admit this!'

Now we have a problem here! Assuming that the first two sentences are true, then if a Fibonian admits that everything he says is a lie, then he must be lying. But if he is lying then he must be telling the truth - and that contradicts the statement. But if the statements are false, then the Fibonian will be telling the truth and, again, we have a contradiction.

A famous paradox was presented by Bertram Russell to illustrate his paradox of set theory in which he showed that there was an inconsistency under certain circumstances. The general theory is a bit difficult to follow, but his example of the barber is easier. It goes along the following lines:

On Russell Island, all the men are clean shaven. There is only one barber, who is also clean shaven. He displays a sign in his window that claims "This barber shaves every man on this island who doesn't shave himself". Now, given that the barber is a man, he must be clean shaven according to the first statement. So there are two possibilities:

1. The barber shaves himself - which can't be true because he claims to shave every man who doesn't shave himself.
2. The barber doesn't shave himself - which would mean that someone else shaves him. But that can only be the barber himself!

So, if the information on the sign is true, we have an impossible situation! Our natural reaction would be to say that the barber's sign was an oversight on his part, but, in the world of mathematics, we build upon some basic 'truths', leading to complicated ideas like 'the set of all infinite sets'. Russell discovered an inconsistency in established theory that gave mathematicians a headache!

Logic

Logic is a wonderful topic that will have instant reward for the young genius who can point out false reasoning in their parents' attempts to justify controversial decisions! A little study will pay dividends in self satisfaction - although don't expect your expert knowledge and analysis to be appreciated!

There are many fun logic puzzles and some of these involve people who always tell the truth and people who always tell lies. Let's start off with a straightforward one:

You are visiting the town of Logiton where the residents may be either liars or truth tellers. You meet a resident in a street and ask him "Are you a liar or a truth teller?" As he replies, a noisy lorry comes past and you don't hear his answer, so you say "Did you say you were a truth teller?" He replies "No, I said I was a liar!"

You deduce which he is by first supposing he is a truth teller and testing this in the story, then suppose he is a liar and test again.

Here's another one for you:

A shopkeeper receives three boxes from his supplier containing jars of jam and honey. One is labelled "JAM (10 JARS)", the second is labelled "HONEY (10 JARS)", the third is labelled "JAM (5 JARS) & HONEY (5 JARS)". Unfortunately, the labels have got mixed up and no box has the correct label. You are allowed to open only one box and examine only one jar from it. Which box do you choose and how are you then able to label each box correctly?

A classic problem, perhaps slightly harder, is that of the prisoner which goes something like this:

A prisoner is being held in a room which has two doors. He knows that one of these leads to freedom while the other leads to the gallows - but he doesn't know which is which! He is allowed to ask one question to one of the two guards. Now, one of the guards always tells the truth and the other always tells lies - but again he doesn't know which one is which. What is the question that he must ask to guarantee freedom?

Logic puzzles involving grids

Your local newsagent will usually have a good stock of puzzle magazines and many of these contain logic puzzles that feature a number of statements, accompanied by a grid. A variety of these puzzles with different levels of difficulty can be found at The Logic Zone's website: http://www.thelogiczone.plus.com/. I have used two of their 'Simple Logic Puzzles' in the following examples. We shall work through the first one, called "on the Shelf", to show the principles involved:

Question:
Five boxes of stationery are on a shelf as shown;

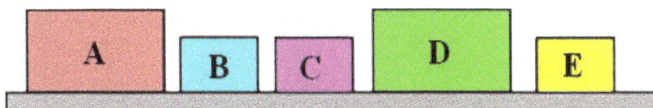

You have to deduce which item is in which box, given the following clues:

1. The box with the pencils is to the right of the box with the pens, which are not in box A.
2. The paperclips are directly to the left of the staples.
3. The notepads are not at either end of the shelf, or next to the staples.

How to solve this puzzle

First, use the given information to write a list of the possible items:
        pencils, pens, paperclips, notepads, staples
Now construct a grid which cross references the items with the shelf positions A-E:

		BOX			
	A	B	C	D	E
PENCILS					
PENS					
PAPERCLIPS					
NOTEPADS					
STAPLES					

Now we are going to use the information given to fill the above grid. We shall put a 1 when we know something is true and a 0 when we know something is false. When we are able to enter a 1 for 'TRUE', all the other entries in that row and column must be 'FALSE", so we can fill them with 0s.

So let's read through those three statements and see what we can put in the grid.

The box with the pencils is to the right of the box with the pens, which are not in box A.

The pens are not in box A, so put a 0 in the grid against A and PENS.

If the pencils are to the right of the pens, then the pencils are not in boxes A or B, so put 0s in the grid.

	BOX				
	A	B	C	D	E
PENCILS	0	0			
PENS	0				
PAPERCLIPS					
NOTEPADS					
STAPLES					

The paperclips are directly to the left of the staples.

So far, we can gather from this that the paperclips cannot be in box E, so enter a 0 against E and paperclips. Also, the staples cannot be in box A if the paperclips are on the left.

The notepads are not at either end of the shelf, or next to the staples.

So we know that the notepads are not in boxes A or E. don't worry about the other details for now.

		BOX				
		A	B	C	D	E
ITEMS	PENCILS	0	0			
	PENS	0				
	PAPERCLIPS					0
	NOTEPADS	0				0
	STAPLES	0				

So, now that we have entered the information from the original three statements, we can look at the grid and enter a TRUE because column A contains 0s apart from the entry for paperclips. This also means that we can enter 0s in the blank positions in that row.

		BOX				
		A	B	C	D	E
ITEMS	PENCILS	0	0			
	PENS	0				
	PAPERCLIPS	1	0	0	0	0
	NOTEPADS	0				0
	STAPLES	0				

Now we have to go back through the statements using the information in the grid to deduce some further facts.

Going back to statement 2: 'The paperclips are directly to the left of the staples.' So the staples must be in Box B. We can put a 1 in the grid against B and Staples. Also, we can put 0s in the rest of the staples row, and in the rest of column B.

	BOX				
	A	B	C	D	E
PENCILS	0	0			
PENS	0	0			
PAPERCLIPS	1	0	0	0	0
NOTEPADS	0	0			0
STAPLES	0	1	0	0	0

(ITEMS)

From statement 3, we know that the notepads are not next to the staples, so they must be in Box D. Again, we put a 1 against notepads and D then fill the rest of the row and column with 0s.

	BOX				
	A	B	C	D	E
PENCILS	0	0		0	
PENS	0	0		0	
PAPERCLIPS	1	0	0	0	0
NOTEPADS	0	0	0	1	0
STAPLES	0	1	0	0	0

(ITEMS)

Nearly there now! You can finish this off by looking back at statement 1. From your final grid, you can read off the contents of each box by looking for the 1 in that column.

Logic puzzles with more components

The above puzzle had two components: the boxes and the stationery. We were able to solve the puzzle using a simple grid. But what if we had more components, such as in the following puzzle (derived from 'Library Books Out', courtesy of The Logic Zone):

Five people have borrowed books on various subjects from the library. By studying the clues below, can you determine the borrower, the title, and the subject of each book? Note that each person has taken out only one book. Full details of names, titles and subjects are shown in the grid.

1. Ben borrowed "Mad Hatters"

2. "Great Toppings" (but not on the subject of Magic) was taken out by Jane

3. Ben was not the man whose subject was Cookery.

4. The book "Food for Thought" was on the subject of Puzzles

5. Pauline borrowed the book on the subject of Cars

6. Dave borrowed "Speedy Tips"

We can't represent these on a simple grid, we would need a 3-dimension grid like a Rubik's cube, but this isn't practical when using a pen and paper. We could draw three grids, representing each layer of the cube, and we represent these as shown:

		TITLE					SUBJECT				
		FOOD FOR THOUGHT	MAD HATTERS	SPEEDY TIPS	GREAT TOPPINGS	TRICKS OF THE TRADE	PUZZLES	CARS	HEADWEAR	MAGIC	COOKERY
BORROWER	BEN										
	CATHY										
	DAVE										
	JANE										
	PAULINE										
SUBJECT	PUZZLES										
	CARS										
	HEADWEAR										
	MAGIC										
	COOKERY										

Now this is not very different from the previous grid, but it involves filling in a few extra 1s or 0s when we have established some information. Here's a bit of a starter:
From clue 1, Ben borrowed "Mad Hatters"
So, we can put a 1 against Ben and "Mad Hatters" and put some 0s in that row and column - but only for the part that we know. As we have not yet found any details about the subject, we shall have to leave these parts of the grid blank for now.

		TITLE					SUBJECT				
		FOOD FOR THOUGHT	MAD HATTERS	SPEEDY TIPS	GREAT TOPPINGS	TRICKS OF THE TRADE	PUZZLES	CARS	HEADWEAR	MAGIC	COOKERY
BORROWER	BEN	0	1	0	0	0					
	CATHY		0								
	DAVE		0								
	JANE		0								
	PAULINE		0								
SUBJECT	PUZZLES										
	CARS										
	HEADWEAR										
	MAGIC										
	COOKERY										

Now look at clue 2: "Great Toppings" (but not on the subject of Magic) was taken out by Jane. So we have three pieces of information here:

"Great Toppings" is not on the subject of Magic - we can put a 0 against Great Toppings" and Magic.

"Great Toppings" was taken out by Jane - we can put a 1 against Great Toppings" and Jane, as well as 0s in that row and column in the inner grid.

Jane did not take out a book on the subject of Magic, so we can put a 0 against Jane and Magic.

		TITLE					SUBJECT				
		FOOD FOR THOUGHT	MAD HATTERS	SPEEDY TIPS	GREAT TOPPINGS	TRICKS OF THE TRADE	PUZZLES	CARS	HEADWEAR	MAGIC	COOKERY
BORROWER	BEN	0	1	0	0	0					
	CATHY		0		0						
	DAVE		0		0						
	JANE	0	0	0	1	0				0	
	PAULINE		0		0						
SUBJECT	PUZZLES										
	CARS										
	HEADWEAR										
	MAGIC				0						
	COOKERY										

You can finish this one off now using clue 3 onwards. Note that clue 3 contains a hidden piece of information. Hint: how many males are there? Also, we know the title of the book that Ben took out, so we can put a 0 against this title and Cookery.

Note that once you have entered all the information from the clues, you will need to use a little thought to progress!

Let's move on to some other ways of untangling logical perplexities.

Solving Logical Puzzles with Diagrams

Sometimes it is useful to draw some simple diagrams to understand the meaning of information given to us. Let's start with a very simple example:

"Some people are taller than 180 centimetres in height"

We think about this in terms of *sets*. First we have the set of **all people** and secondly, we have the set of **people who are taller than 180 centimetres**. These could be represented as shown:

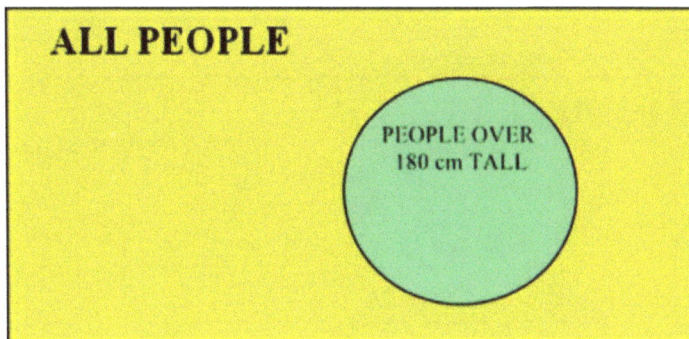

From the diagram, we can see that the set of people who are over 180 cm tall are within the set of all people (as we would expect!) Now let's take some facts for a typical case and see how we might represent them in the diagram.

- John's height is 175 cm

- Alice's height is 162 cm

- Ben's height is 190 cm

- Joan's height is 172 cm

- Brenda's height is 184 cm

- Henry's height is 164 cm

How can we use the diagram for this information? All the people who are taller than 180cm belong in the green circle while all the others are in the yellow area:

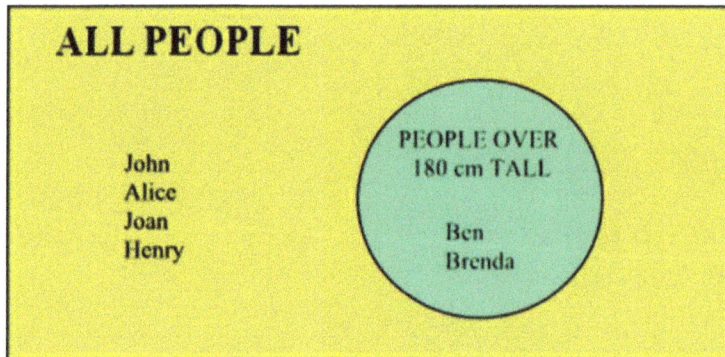

So we can see that Ben and Brenda are amongst the set of all people, but they have the special property of being in a *subset* that describes people who are taller than 180 cm. Now let's extend this a bit further and introduce another set that describes people whose height is less than 185 cm. So that's everyone on our list apart from Ben. Note that Brenda belongs to both sets.

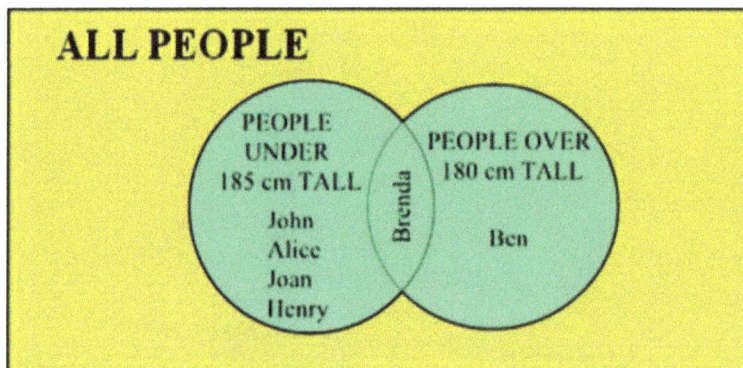

We say that Brenda belongs to the **intersection** of the two sets. All the people on our list would form the **union** of the two sets. Note that there are no people who don't belong to either set.

We call these **Venn diagrams** - named after John Venn, although his work in 1880 was based on **Euler diagrams** devised by the Swiss mathematician, Leonhard Euler (1707 - 1783).

So how can we make some practical use of Venn diagrams? Well, they can help us sort out complicated information. Take a simple example:

At the Alpha Sports Academy, all 250 students take part in one or more sports. 70 students play cricket and 125 students play football. 25 students play both cricket and football. How many students do not play either cricket or football?

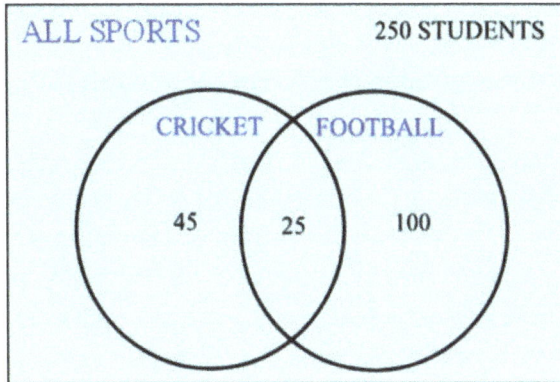

From the diagram, we see that 45 students play cricket only, 100 students play football only and 25 play both cricket and football. In total there are 170 students that play either cricket or football. There are a total of 250 students, so 80 of them do not play either cricket or football.

Here's one for you:

There are 10 people at a party. Some are eating cake, some are drinking squash, and some are eating cake and drinking squash. If 3 people are eating cake and 5 people drinking squash, how many are both eating cake and drinking squash?

An interesting example of a Venn diagram occurs when we mix red, green and blue lights on a black background (the RGB colour model).

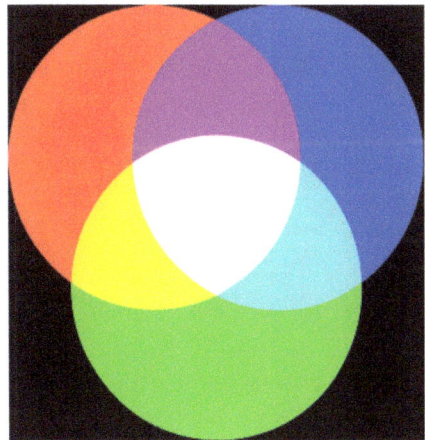

FURTHER QUESTIONS

1. Seven tourists arrive together at an hotel one evening. They each want a separate room but there are only six rooms available. But the manager says "No problem!" He takes the first two tourists and puts the first one in the first room and asks the second to wait in the same room for a moment. He then takes the third guest to the second room, the fourth to the third room, the fifth to the fourth room, and the sixth to the fifth room. He then goes back to the first room, gets the seventh man and puts him in the sixth room. Everyone has been accommodated! But how?

2. Jane keeps a regular diary that includes her total monthly spending. One day she looked at her diary of 5 years ago and it showed that her total outgoings were £1000 per month. She then looked at her current outgoings and found they were £1500 per month for exactly the same items - an increase of 50%. But, she reasoned that because she had received a 10% increase every year in her income, it amounted to a 50% increase over the 5 years and so she was no better or worse off as a result. If Jane asked you for your opinion, what would you tell her?

3. A convicted murderer had been sentenced to death by hanging. The judge announced that the execution would take place one day in the following week (Monday to Friday), but that the exact day would not be revealed until the actual day of the hanging and it would come as a surprise. The prisoner returned to his cell and thought about the judge's remarks and reasoned that the execution can't be on the Friday because if he hasn't been hanged by Thursday, the hanging would have to be the next day so it would not be a surprise. Similarly, he reasoned that the execution would not be on Thursday, because Friday had already been eliminated and if he had not been hanged by Wednesday night, the hanging must occur on Thursday, making a Thursday hanging not a surprise either. By applying the same logic, he reasoned that the execution could not be on Wednesday, Tuesday or Monday. He concluded happily that the hanging would not take place at all. However, to his great surprise, the executioner arrived at the prisoner's cell on Wednesday of the following week. Apparently, the judge's remarks had been correct!

4. Zeno's paradox: a hare and a tortoise agree to take part in a race and, as the hare can run fastest, the tortoise is given a 100 metre lead. They both run at constant, but different speeds. The race starts and the hare runs up to the 100 metre point, but by this time the tortoise has moved on some distance. By the time the hare gets to the point where the tortoise had reached, the tortoise had moved further ahead. Again, when the hare arrives at this point the tortoise has moved on. This situation must always continue and so the hare can never overtake the tortoise! Can you explain?

5. A bat and a ball costs £11. If the bat costs £10 more than the ball, how much does the ball cost?

6. Jack is looking at a photograph and says "Brothers and sisters have I none, but this man's father is my father's son". What relation is Jack to the man in the photograph?

7. A man lives on the tenth floor of a block of flats. Every morning, he takes the lift down to the ground floor and goes to his work. When he comes back after work, if it is a rainy day he goes to his floor directly, otherwise he goes to the seventh floor and walks up three flights of stairs to his flat. What might explain this?

8. John, Anne, Diane and Ben each live in a flat in a block that has only 4 floors. They live on separate floors and each of their doors is a different colour: red, green, blue and yellow. Can you work out who lives where and the colour of their door given the following:

   - The red door is on a higher floor than Anne
   - The green door is one floor above Diane
   - Diane lives 2 floors above Anne
   - The yellow door is on a higher floor than John

9. A small town ran an evening cookery class for 20 residents. One evening, they were taught how to cook two different dishes: omelette and pizza and afterwards, the instructor conducted a survey of people's likings. 14 said that they liked omelette and 10 said that they liked pizza. There were 2 students who did not like either. How many of them liked both omelette and pizza?

10. A man has to cross a river in his canoe. He has a wolf, a goat, and a cabbage that he needs to take with him but the canoe is only big enough for him to take just one of these with him on any crossing. Unfortunately, if he leaves the wolf with the goat, the wolf will eat the goat. Similarly, if he leaves the goat with the cabbage, the goat will eat the cabbage. How does he get all three safely across to the other side of the river?

Answers to Questions for Chapter Five

Dubious Percentages
Final price of cake = £2.46

Logic

He takes a jar from the labelled 'Jam and Honey'. Let's suppose it is jam. He then takes the label from the box labelled 'Jam' and puts it on this box. He now has 2 boxes, but only one of them has a label and because he knows that this is incorrect, it must belong to the other box. He can then put the 'Jam and Honey' label on the remaining box.

The prisoner asks either one of the guards "If you were the other guard which door would you tell me to take to gain my freedom?"

Five boxes of stationery

BOX A	BOX B	BOX C	BOX D	BOX E
PAPERCLIPS	STAPLES	PENS	NOTEPADS	PENCILS

Library Books

		TITLE					SUBJECT			
		FOOD FOR THOUGHT	MAD HATTERS	SPEEDY TIPS	GREAT TOPPINGS	TRICKS OF THE TRADE	PUZZLES	CARS	HEADWEAR	MAGIC	COOKERY
BORROWER	BEN	0	1	0	0	0	0	0	0	1	0
	CATHY	1	0	0	0	0	1	0	0	0	0
	DAVE	0	0	1	0	0	0	0	0	0	1
	JANE	0	0	0	1	0	0	0	1	0	0
	PAULINE	0	0	0	0	1	0	1	0	0	0
SUBJECT	PUZZLES	1	0	0	0	0					
	CARS	0	0	0	0	1					
	HEADWEAR	0	0	0	1	0					
	MAGIC	0	1	0	0	0					
	COOKERY	0	0	1	0	0					

Answers to Further Questions

1. If you are in doubt, draw a little diagram with 7 tourists and 6 rooms. Follow the directions and pay careful attention to what happens to the 7th tourist!

2. Over the period, Jane's outgoings did rise by 50%, but her income rose by 10% per year so, each year, she was receiving 10% more of what she had the previous year - an overall increase of approximately 61%. But that was only looking at her fixed outgoings. Suppose she originally had an income of £2000 per month then her disposable income would be £2000 - £1000 = £1000 at the start. But at the end, her income would be £3220 per month and her outgoings were £1500 per month, so her final disposable income was £1720 per month, so in this respect, she was 70% better off!

3. The fault in the reasoning is that, for example, if he hadn't been hanged by Wednesday then he wouldn't be hanged on Thursday or Friday. Of course, this is untrue, his argument only applied to Friday when all other possibilities had been eliminated.

4. This is a nice trick that involves taking you down a wrong method of reasoning involving an infinite number of diminishing steps.

5. The bat costs £10.50 and the ball costs £0.50.

6. The man in the photograph is Jack's son. This man's father would be Jack who would be the son of Jack's father.

7. He is a short man who cannot reach the lift buttons beyond floor 7 (we assume that they are arranged in a vertical order corresponding to the physical layout of the flats). When it it raining, he has his umbrella and can therefore press the higher buttons.

8. John has the red door on floor 2, Anne has the blue door on floor 1, Diane has the yellow door on floor 3 and Ben has the green door on floor 4.

9. Eight like only omelette, four like only pizza, **six like both omelette and pizza** (total 18). Two do not like either, giving a total of 20 students.

10. He first takes the goat across, knowing that, as a carnivore, the wolf won't eat the cabbage. He comes back and collects the cabbage and takes it to the other side but brings back the goat. He then takes the wolf across, comes back and returns with the goat.

Chapter 6   Logic and Computers

Computers use binary numbers to represent numbers, text and even graphical images. Their whole working is based upon binary numbers because a binary digit, or *bit*, can easily be represented in an OFF/ON way corresponding to 0 and 1. We think that computers are clever, but they're not really! They can do clever things but, at their heart, they are only doing some very simple operations with tiny electronic circuits called *logic gates* and binary numbers!

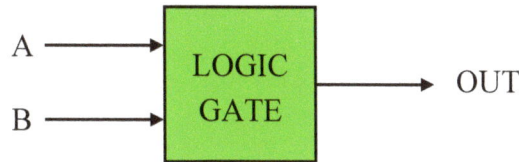

Logic Gates

Logic gates typically have 1 or 2 inputs and they have just one output. So, imagine a couple of wires connected to the inputs, labelled A and B. Each wire can be in one of two states: high voltage or low voltage, representing 1 and 0 respectively. Now we can forget about the voltages and just talk in terms of 1s and 0s as the signals that are fed to our logic gates. Similarly the output from a gate can be only 1 or 0.

The Basic Gates and Truth Tables

Computers use thousands of logic gates that perform the logical operations of **AND, OR, EOR** (exclusive OR) and **NOT**. If we use **1** to represent **TRUE** and **0** to represent **FALSE**, we can describe the functions of these gates by **truth tables** as follows:

NOT	
A	$\overline{A}$
1	0
0	1

AND		
A	B	A.B
0	0	0
0	1	0
1	0	0
1	1	1

OR		
A	B	A+B
0	0	0
0	1	1
1	0	1
1	1	1

EOR		
A	B	A⊕B
0	0	0
0	1	1
1	0	1
1	1	0

The simplest gate is the NOT gate. It has just one input and, like all the other logic gates, has just one output. If we put a 0 in, we get a 1 out and if we put a 1 in we get a 0 out. Not surprisingly, the NOT gate is also known as an INVERTER. It is usually drawn as shown.

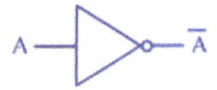

A ———▷o— $\overline{A}$

The other gates have two inputs that can each be a 1 or a 0. The particular output is described in the relevant truth table as shown above. The AND gate with inputs A and B outputs 1 if both A AND B are 1s. The OR gate outputs 1 if either A or B (or both) is a 1.

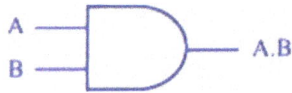

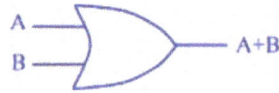

A
B ——— A.B

A
B ——— A+B

The EXCLUSIVE OR (EOR) gate is like the OR gate except that it excludes the case when both inputs are 1s when it outputs 0.

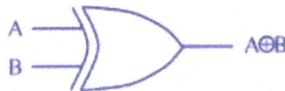

A
B ——— A⊕B

Practical Usage

So how might these logic gates be of practical use? One thing we might want to do is to add together two numbers. Let's just remind ourselves of what happens when we add two normal (denary) numbers:

5 + 7 = 12 No surprise there then! But how do we do 58 + 64 or even 429 + 763? Just have a go at those on piece of paper and have a think about what you did.

Done that? OK, what you should have realised is that when we are adding two numbers, we add corresponding digits and generate a SUM digit and a CARRY digit for each pair of digits. For example:

```
      5   8                5   8                0   5   8
  +   6   4            +   6   4            +   0   6   4
      -----------          1                    1
          2 (SUM)          -----------          -----------------
          1 (CARRY)        2   2                1   2   2
                       1 (CARRY)
```

Result 122

So we see that addition involves adding pairs of digits and generating a SUM and a CARRY for the first (rightmost) pair. After that, we add three digits: the two digits from our original numbers and the CARRY from the previous stage - but we still generate a SUM and a CARRY.

Is this is all sounding a bit complicated? It's not really - but you need to understand what you are doing when you add two numbers together, so if any of that is not clear, try adding a few more numbers together using the 'mechanical' approach above until you are quite clear about SUMs and CARRYs.

Now I need you to put your binary number hat on for a moment ..... all in place? Right, let's go!

The Half Adder

Now what are the possibilities when we add two binary digits?

```
        0              0            1            1
  +     0              1            0            1
       ---            ---          ----         ----
        0              1            1           10
```

Or, in more detail:

```
        0              0            1            1
  +     0              1            0            1
       ---            ---          ----         ----
      SUM 0         SUM  1       SUM  1       SUM  0
      CARRY 0       CARRY 0      CARRY 0      CARRY 1
```

Let's label the first digit as A and the second one as B.

```
        A
  +     B
       ---
       SUM
       CARRY
```

If we could make a device to take two binary digits: A and B, and output two digits: SUM and CARRY, we are on our way towards making a computer! Well, let's imagine that we can produce such a device and we'll call it a *binary half adder* (I'll explain this in a minute).

We can start by thinking of it as a box with two inputs: A and B, and two outputs: SUM and CARRY as shown below:

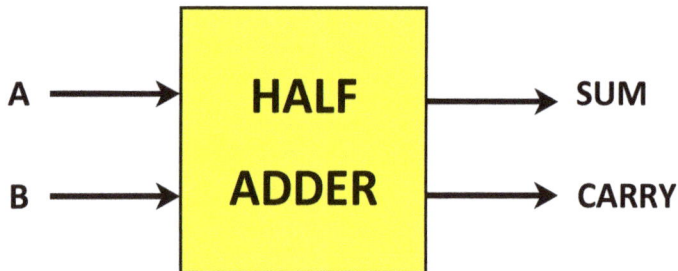

Now let's draw up a table that defines what each output should be for any combination of the inputs.

A	B	Sum	Carry
0	0	0	0
0	1	1	0
1	0	1	0
1	1	0	1

Look at the column labelled 'Sum'. Have you seen it before somewhere? Have a look back at our earlier truth table for the basic gates just to remind yourself. Yes- it's the Exclusive OR for A and B (A EOR B).

Now what about the column labelled 'Carry'? We've seen that one before as well - it's the AND function for A and B (A AND B).

If we were to connect up some logic gates, our circuit would look like:

Hurrah! We have created a means of doing simple addition!

The Full Adder

Now why did I give it that strange title 'binary **half** adder'? Well, it's because it only works for the rightmost pair of digits when we are adding. Try adding 11 and 11 in binary (in denary that is 3+3 = 6).

We start by adding the rightmost digits which gives the sum 0 and the carry 1:

```
        1     1
+       1     1
      -----------
              0
      carry 1
```

Now we proceed to add the next pair of digits to the left of the first pair. We have 1 + 1 as before, but this time we also have to add the carry of 1. So our adder circuit won't quite do because this time we have three inputs: A, B and Carry In and, as before, we have two outputs: Sum and Carry Out. This gives us the 'binary **full** adder', as shown:

Once again, we would draw up a truth table to help us work out what we need in terms of logic gates. It's a bit more complicated this time, but I'll start you off and see if you can complete the table.

INPUTS			OUTPUTS	
A	B	C in	SUM	C out
0	0	0		
0	0	1		
0	1	0		
0	1	1		
1	0	0		
1	0	1		
1	1	0		
1	1	1		

Now, it is possible to work out the logic circuit from the completed truth table, but there's a simpler way. Think about adding the numbers using the following steps.

1.   Add together the digits A and B using a half-adder as before. This will generate a sum digit S1 and a carry digit C1.

2.   Next, add the Carry In to the sum S1 that we have just generated. Again, we only need a half-adder for this and we generate a final Sum digit, S2 and another Carry digit, C2.

3.   In steps 1 or 2 above, a carry of 1 may be generated by either step, but not both. So the final carry, Cout = C1 OR C2.

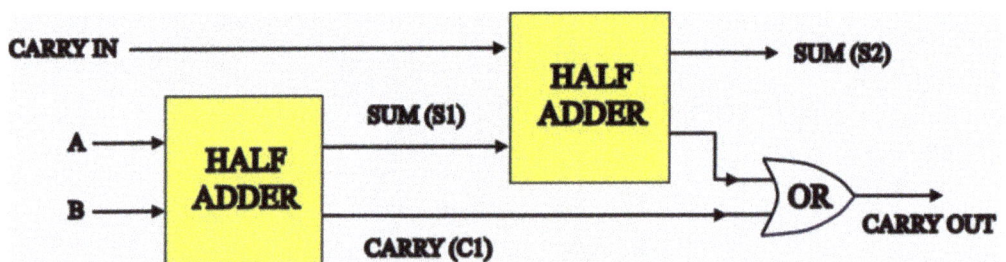

So all you have to do is substitute the block labelled 'HALF ADDER' with the circuits showing the actual logic gates and you have the complete circuit for a binary full adder. Have a go at drawing the complete circuit for yourself - see 'ANSWERS' to check your diagram.

Of course, in a real computer you would be adding together two 8-digit binary numbers, so we would need a full adder for each pair of binary digits (although we would only need a half adder for the rightmost digits).

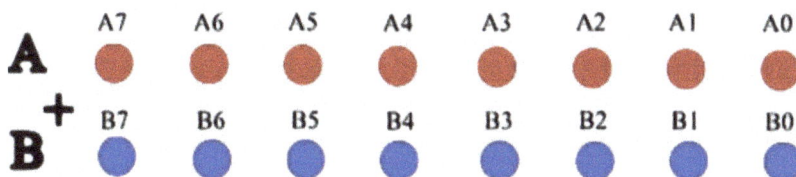

Can you work out how to connect each pair of digits to adders? Use block diagrams for the adders.

FURTHER QUESTIONS

1. What is the output, B, from the following circuit:

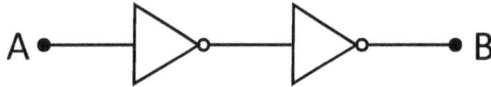

2. A logic circuit has 3 inputs A, B, and C. It has a single output, X which is determined by the rule: X = (A AND B) OR C. Draw the logic circuit.

3. Draw the truth table for the circuit in question 2. Hint: the possible inputs will be the same as for the full adder. Create a column for A AND B, call this D then calculate D OR C.

4. Two other logic gates are NAND and NOR, short for NOT AND and NOT OR respectively. As you might expect, the NAND gate is essentially an AND gate followed by a NOT. Similarly the NOR gate is an OR gate followed by a NOT. If the NAND and the NOR each have two inputs A and B, they have a single output, X, can you draw the truth tables?

5. There are two very useful rules known as De Morgan's Laws. These are: NOT(A AND B) = (NOT A) OR (NOT B) and NOT(A OR B) = (NOT A) AND (NOT B). Can you prove these by drawing up two truth tables in each case?

6. Draw the logic circuit for X = {(NOT A) AND B} OR {A AND (NOT B)}

7. Draw up the truth table for the circuit in question 6. To do this, give a label to each gate's output and create a corresponding column in the truth table. What do you notice about X?

8. The ones complement of a binary number is formed by changing all the 0s to 1s and all the 1s to 0s. The twos complement of a binary number is formed by adding 1 to the ones complement. Using 4 binary digits, what is the binary for 3? Find its twos complement.

9. Computers use the twos complement to perform subtraction. Again using 4 binary digits, calculate 9 - 3 by **adding** the twos complement of 3 to the binary value for 9 and ignoring the final carry digit.

10. Can you draw an outline design for a 4 bit subtraction circuit?

Answers to Questions for Chapter Six

Truth table for a full adder:

A	B	Cin	SUM	Cout
0	0	0	0	0
0	0	1	1	0
0	1	0	1	0
0	1	1	0	1
1	0	0	1	0
1	0	1	0	1
1	1	0	0	1
1	1	1	1	1

Circuit for a Full Adder:

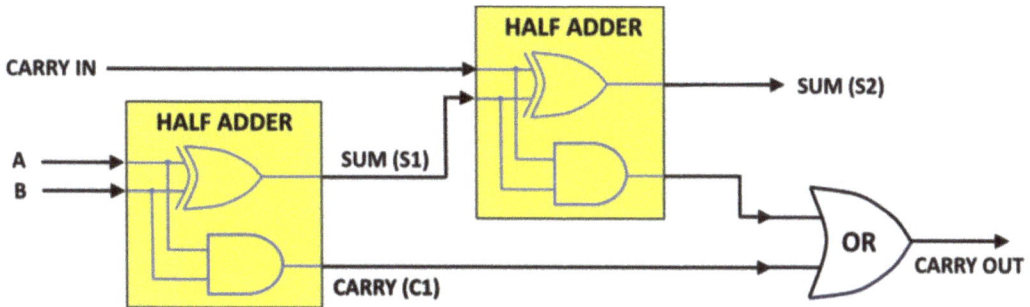

An 8 Bit Binary Adder:

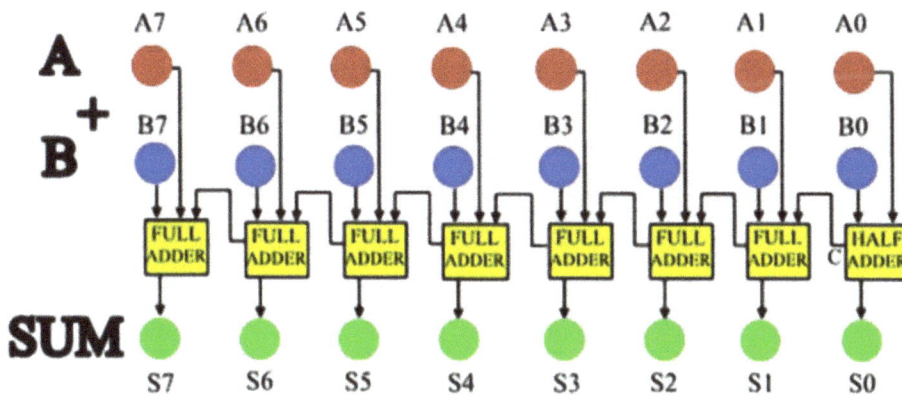

Answers to Further Questions

1. B = A (You can prove this with a truth table)

2.

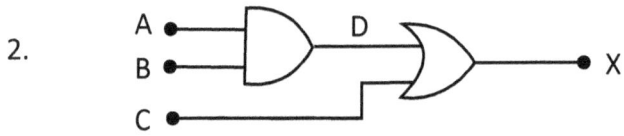

3.

A	B	C	D	X
0	0	0	0	0
0	0	1	0	1
0	1	0	0	0
0	1	1	0	1
1	0	0	0	0
1	0	1	0	1
1	1	0	1	1
1	1	1	1	1

4. NAND:

A	B	A AND B	X
0	0	0	1
0	1	0	1
1	0	0	1
1	1	1	0

NOR:

A	B	A OR B	X
0	0	0	1
0	1	1	0
1	0	1	0
1	1	1	0

5.

A	B	A AND B	NOT(A AND B)
0	0	0	1
0	1	0	1
1	0	0	1
1	1	1	0

A	B	NOT A	NOT B	(NOT A) OR (NOT B)
0	0	1	1	1
0	1	1	0	1
1	0	0	1	1
1	1	0	0	0

A	B	A OR B	NOT(A OR B)
0	0	0	1
0	1	1	0
1	0	1	0
1	1	1	0

A	B	NOT A	NOT B	(NOT A) AND (NOT B)
0	0	1	1	1
0	1	1	0	0
1	0	0	1	0
1	1	0	0	0

6.

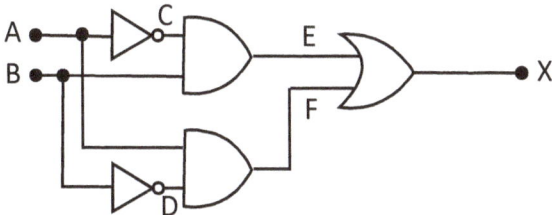

7.

A	B	C	D	E	F	X
0	0	1	1	0	0	0
0	1	1	0	1	0	1
1	0	0	1	0	1	1
1	1	0	0	0	0	0

X is the EXCLUSIVE OR FUNCTION

8. Using 4 binary digits, 3 would be 0011

The ones complement of 3 is 1100, the twos complement is 1101.

9. 9 - 3 is performed as 9 + twos complement of 3 (ignoring final carry digit)

1001 + 1101 = (1)0110

0110 is 6 in denary

10. We can get the ones complement of a binary number by using a NOT gate on each bit of the number. So, for a 4 bit number we would have:

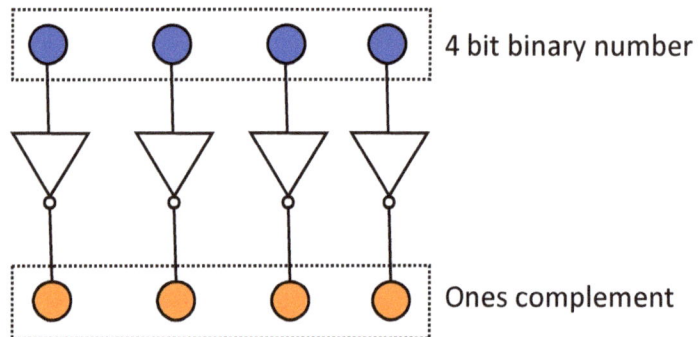

4 bit binary number

Ones complement

Now, we know that the twos complement is formed by adding 1 to the ones complement and we are going to add the twos complement to the other number. But we already have a circuit for adding two numbers together, so we could use this to first add 1 to the ones complement and then add the result to the other number.

But with a slight modification, we could add the ones complement directly to the other number while bringing in the extra 1 as a carry-in. So, in our original adding circuit, we use full adders for all the bits and set the first carry-in to 1. The outline circuit is shown below:

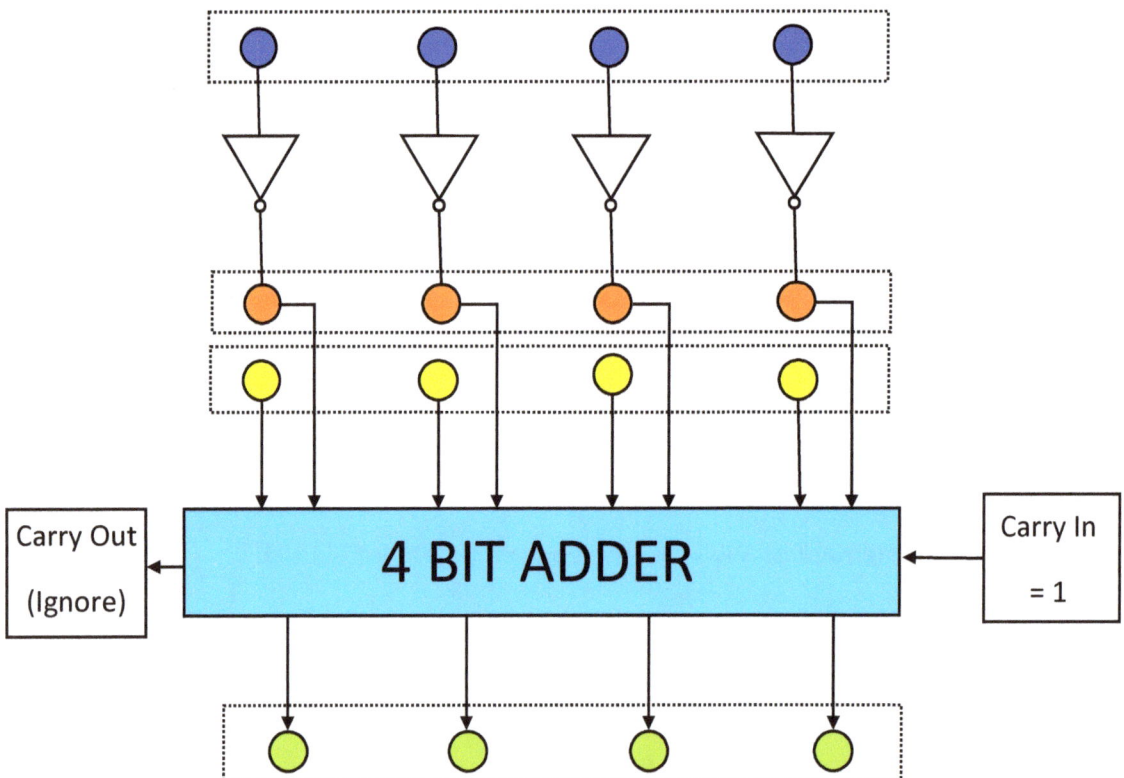

Carry Out

(Ignore)

4 BIT ADDER

Carry In

= 1

Chapter 7: The Euler Number

There's a number that we call **e** which is roughly equal to 2.718 and it has a very special place in mathematics. It is called the 'Euler Number' after the famous Swiss mathematician Leonhard Euler about 3 centuries ago. The choice of the letter e and the first letter of his surname are probably coincidental!

We find that e crops up frequently when we analyse things that occur naturally. For example, the spread of a disease may be directly linked to the number of people who are currently infected. We can write down an equation which we call a 'mathematical model' of this situation and it turns out that the solution to this involves our old friend e.

Back to Factorials

Talking of old friends, do you remember factorials? We used the exclamation mark (!) after a number to indicate that we multiply it by all numbers below it down to 1.

For example: $6! = 6 \times 5 \times 4 \times 3 \times 2 \times 1$

For convenience, we define $1! = 1$ and $0! = 1$.

Now it turns out that e can be expressed in terms of factorials:

$e = 1/0! + 1/1! + 1/2! + 1/3! + 1/4! + 1/5! + \ldots\ldots$ (for ever)

That's pretty neat, isn't it? Have a go at calculating it yourself up as far as 1/7! - what do you get?

It should come out to be just over 2.71825 - which isn't far off! Did you spot a short cut in calculating the factorials? The factorial of any number is that number multiplied by the factorial of the number below it. So if, for example, you've calculated 5! you can use the fact that $6! = 6 \times 5!$ Because:

$6! = 6 \times 5 \times 4 \times 3 \times 2 \times 1 = 6 \times (5 \times 4 \times 3 \times 2 \times 1) = 6 \times 5!$

In general, $N! = N \times (N-1)!$ This is rather nice because it leads us to the idea of _**recursion**_, where something can be defined in terms of itself.

For example, if we had a calculating machine called FACTORIAL then we could define:

FACTORIAL(N) = N x FACTORIAL(N-1)
for N greater than 1 and FACTORIAL(1) = 1.

In fact, we use this sort of idea in computer programs, but it has to be done with care because if you make a mistake it can go on referring to itself for ever!

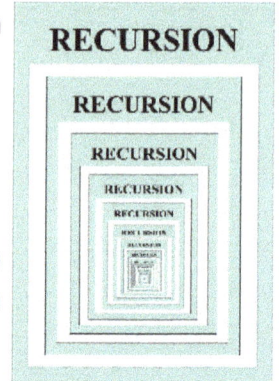

Anyway, back to e. It is a number (like π) with decimal places that go on for ever and doesn't end up in a repeating sequence of digits:

e = 2.718281828459045235360287413527............

An easy way of remembering the first few digits is to split it up as follows:

e = 2.7 1828 1828 45 90 45

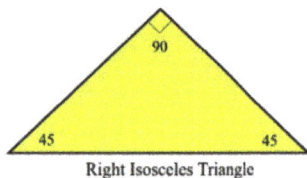

So the 2.7 is easy to remember and then we repeat the 1828. The next three pairs of digits 45, 90, 45 are the same as the angles of a 'right isosceles triangle' (a right angled with two equal sides and since the angles of a triangle add up to 180°, we have 45°, 90°, and 45°).

Right Isosceles Triangle

Before we go on, let us remind ourselves of what we mean by *a power of a number*. In its basic sense, it is the number of times a number is multiplied by itself.

For example: 10 to the power 2 = 10 x 10. We would write this as 10^2.

So 10^4 = 10 x 10 x 10 x 10 = 10,000.

The power is usually called the *index* or *exponent* of the number. The number being raised to a power is often called the *base*. Of course, the base doesn't have to be 10 e.g. it could be 7 so that we might have 7^2 = 7 x 7 = 49. More on this later, but let's get back to e.

Another way of Calculating e

Another way of obtaining e is to calculate $(1 + 1/n)^n$ for a very large value of n. Let's look at what this comes out to be for a few values of n:

n=10: $(1 + 1/10)^{10}$ =   2.59374
n=100: $(1 + 1/100)^{100}$ =   2.70481
n=1000: $(1 + 1/1000)^{1000}$ = 2.71692

and, in the limit, as n tends to infinity, we get:

$$e = 2.71828182845904523536028747135527............$$

This definition of e is perhaps less useful than our method using factorials but it has a similarity to the formula used for loans and investments and with a little manipulation, we can get an equation involving e for certain financial schemes.

e and logarithms

The number e is in everyday use by mathematicians, engineers, and other scientists in the context of **logarithms**. Historically, scientific calculations were hampered by the sheer amount of time that it took to perform the arithmetic - particularly multiplications and divisions. It was not until early in the 17th century when a breakthrough was made when the Scottish laird and mathematician, John Napier, introduced his *Naperian logarithms,* on which he had been working for some time. Soon after that, an Oxford professor called Henry Briggs simplified Napier's idea and established the *'common'* logarithms that were to be used in calculations until electronic calculators emerged in the late 1960s.

Logarithms use the nice idea that it is easier to add two numbers rather than multiply them. This was also the basis of the *slide rule*, again widely used prior to the electronic calculator.

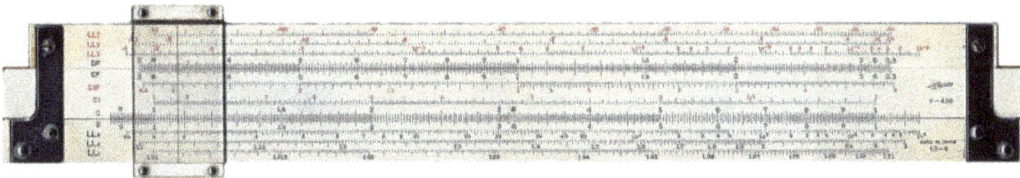

Let's just return to powers of 10 for a moment. We have seen that we can write 100 as 10 x 10 or 10^2. Similarly, we can write 1000 as 10 x 10 x 10 or 10^3.

Now, if we want to calculate 100 x 1000 = (10 x 10) x (10 x 10 x 10) = 100, 000 or 10^5. So $10^2 \times 10^3 = 10^5$, in other words to **multiply** two numbers we **add** their exponents as long as they have a common base number. That is $10^2 \times 10^3 = 10^{(2+3)}$ and that's how logarithms work. Any number can be expressed as a power of 10 if we can extend our ideas to exponents with values like 0.2 and so on. For example:

$2 \times 3 = 10^{0.3010} \times 10^{0.4771} = 10^{(0.3010 + 0.4771)} = 10^{0.7781} = 6$ (which we find from a table of *antilogarithms*)

The logarithm of a number is the power that we have to raise 10 to in order to get that number. So, in the above example the log of 2 is 0.3010, the log of 3 is 0.4771.

Question: what is the log of 6?

A shorthand way of writing 'common logarithm' is $\log_{10}$ for example: $\log_{10}(3) = 0.4771$
So far, we have looked at **common logarithms** which use 10 as a base. But we could use almost any number as a base, including our old friend e. For example:

$2 \times 3 = e^{0.6931} \times e^{1.0986} = e^{(0.6931 + 1.0986)} = e^{1.7917} = 6$

When we use logarithms with the base e, we call them **natural logarithms**.

Question: what is the natural log of 3?

When we wish to make clear that we are using natural logarithms, we write $\log_e$ or just ln for example $\ln(2) = 0.6931$

One example of where a natural logarithm appears is if we draw the curve for y = 1/x and work out the area beneath the curve between x= 1 and x=a. this turns out to be ln(a). An example is shown below for the area beneath the curve y = 1/x between x =1 and x=2.5 for which the area is ln(2.5) = 0.916 square units (approx).

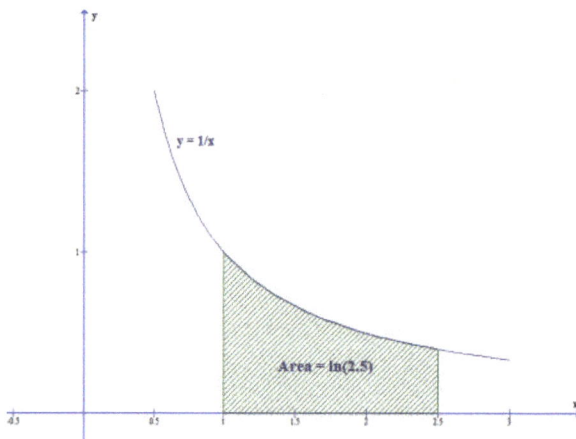

You can check this yourself by working out the approximate area. Let's start by using a calculator to work out a few values of y = 1/x for some of the values of x.

x	1	1.5	2	2.5
y = 1/x	1	0.667	0.5	0.4

Now get a sheet of graph paper because we are going to draw a graph similar to the one above, but limited to the shaded area.

As with all graphs, we start off by drawing the x and y axes: the x axis is the horizontal line and the y axis is the vertical line (see the graph above). Choose your scale to make it as large as possible.

Note that, in this case, we start the x axis at x=1. So far, you should have something that looks like this:

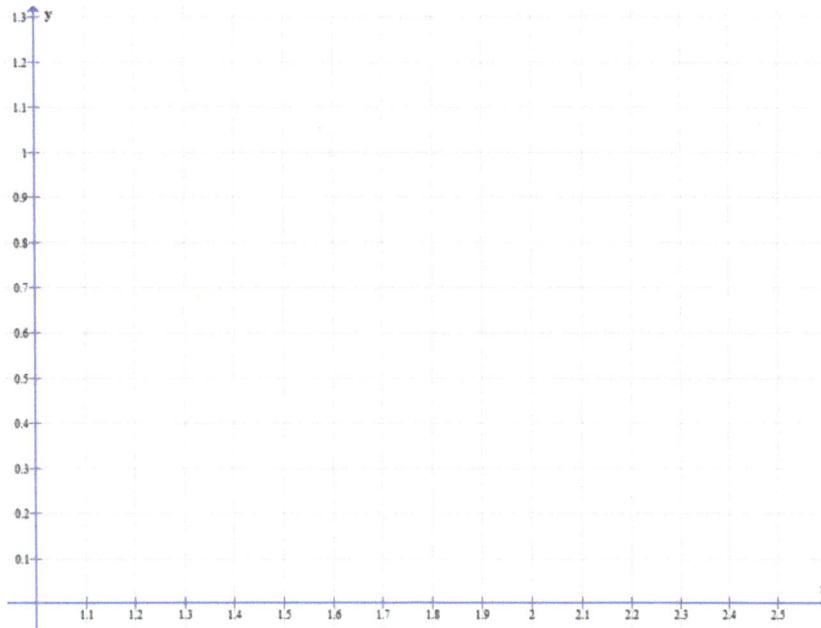

On your graph, plot the points from the table above on a sheet of graph paper. Then join up the points with a smooth curve. Hint: to draw a smooth curve, use your elbow as a pivot and place your graph paper so that when you rotate your arm, your pencil travels above the points on the curve. Adjust as necessary until one smooth movement will go through all the points.

Alternatively you can buy something known as a flexicurve which is basically a thick bendable rod that you can adjust to help you draw curves.

Your graph should now look like this:

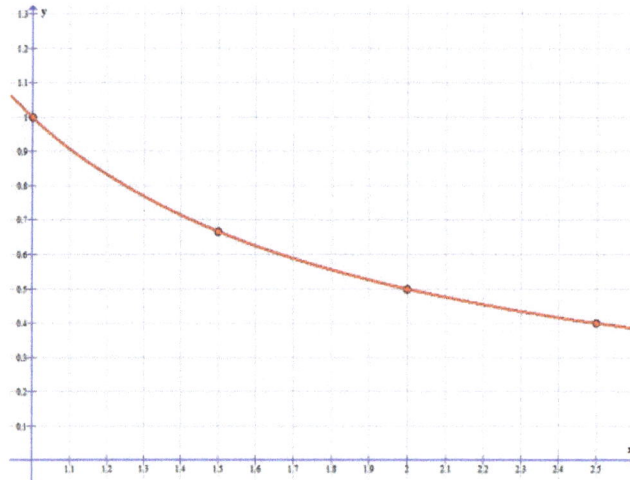

Now draw three trapeziums on your graph as shown below:

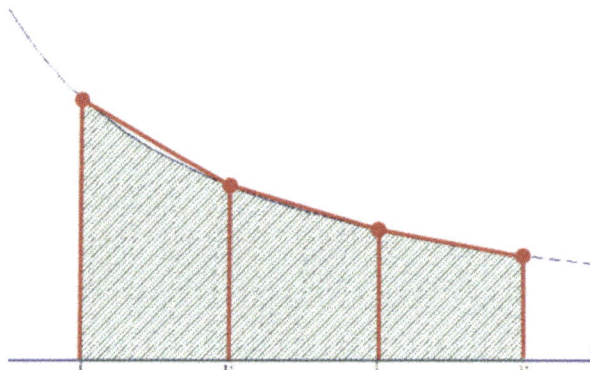

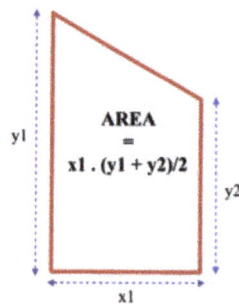

AREA
=
x1 . (y1 + y2)/2

94

Then calculate the approximate area by working out the area for each trapezium and adding the three areas together.

What do answer do you get? How does it compare to the true value of 0.916 square units?

You can get a more accurate result by drawing more trapeziums e.g. twice as many with half the width of the previous ones. Have a go and see how you get on.

You may have realised by now that it isn't necessary to draw the graph to do this. Instead we can draw up a table of values. For example the first attempt would look like:

x	1	1.5	2	2.5
y = 1/x	1	0.667	0.5	0.4
Area	0.417	0.292	0.225	

Total Area = 0.417 + 0.292 + 0.225 = 0.934 square units

Looking back at the graph where we drew the trapeziums, we can see why this is an overestimate because the top of each trapezium is slightly above the curve y = 1/x. If we increase the number of trapeziums, the tops more closely follow the curve and we get a more accurate answer. In fact, we can get an estimate of the accuracy of our answer if, when we halve the trapezium width each time, we compare successive estimates.

e raised to a power

What does the graph of e^x look like? Try plotting a few values of $y = e^x$ on a sheet of graph paper. It might help to draw up a table of values first, for example (fill in the missing values using a calculator, round your answers to 2 decimal places):

x	-2	-1.5	-1	-0.5	0	0.5	1
y = e^x	0.14	0.22					2.72

Plot the values from the above table as a set of dots on a sheet of graph paper and join them up with a smooth curve.

Now let's try to get a more accurate curve by plotting more points. Start off by drawing up a table like the one above but with values of x going from -2.4 to + 1.4 in steps of 0.2

Next plot your graph on a sheet of graph paper choosing your scales to use as much of the sheet as possible. Plot each point in turn and then join them up with a nice smooth curve. You should end up with a graph that looks like the one shown below:

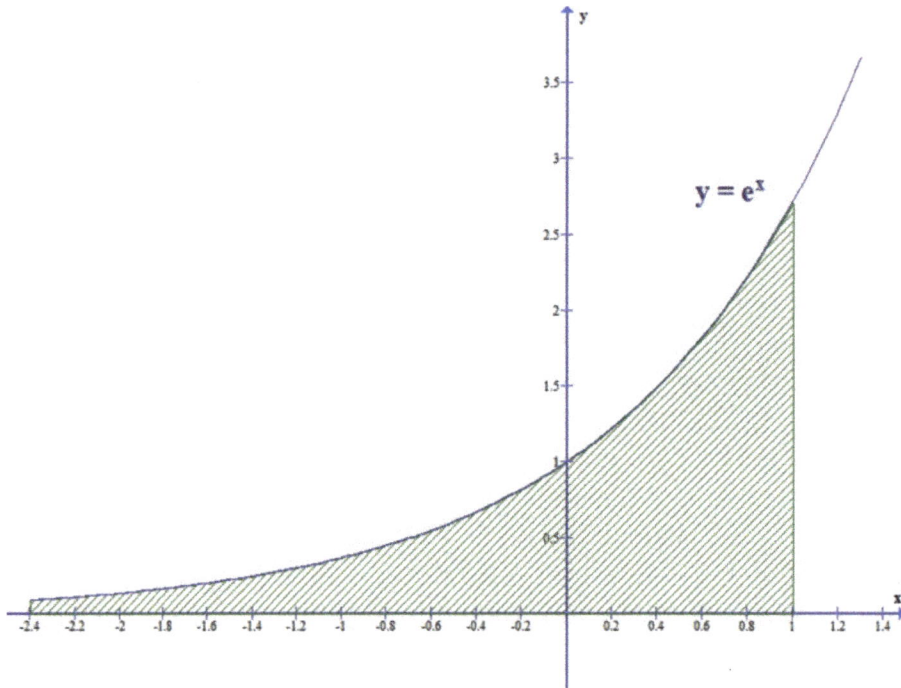

As we mentioned at the start, e occurs naturally, particularly in forms like $y = e^x$ which could represent the spread of a disease. Another example is the increase in bacteria as food ages - the curves are used to set 'Use-by' dates at points where the curve is relatively flat. We would avoid steep parts of the curve where bacteria are multiplying rapidly - unless we want a seriously bad stomach upset! In reality, there is a stage with bacteria before exponential growth begins, called the *lag phase*, and we would try to set our 'Use-by' date in this region.

Gradients

We are often interested in the steepness of a curve and we call this its **gradient** or its **slope**. This is simply a measure of how much the curve rises over a given horizontal distance.

The curve for e^x has the strange property that its gradient at any point x is equal to e^x. You can check this for yourself. First let's look at how you can estimate the gradient of a curve at any point, x.

We can start off with a simple example of a straight road on a steep hill which might look like this from a side view:

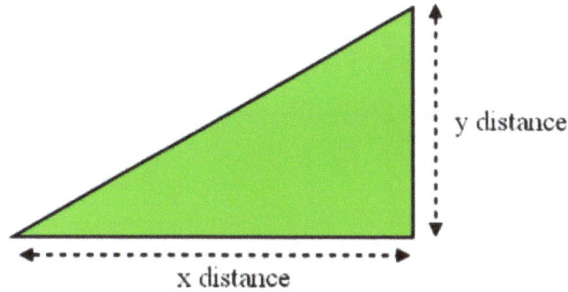

The gradient is equal to the y distance divided by the x distance.

Question: What is the gradient of the hill shown below:

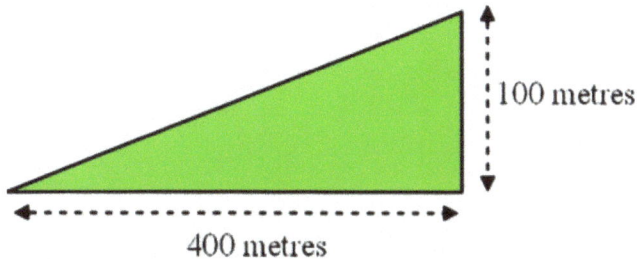

You can see examples of this on road signs warning of a steep hill:

Road signs usually express the gradient as a percentage. This is simply 100 times the decimal value. For example, if our hill went up 50 metres over a horizontal distance of 250 metres, the gradient would be 50/250 = 1/5 = 0.2 or 20%. In mathematics, we usually just express the gradient as a decimal number.

If we generalise our idea of the road going up a hill to a straight line on a piece of graph paper, this will help us to understand other lines such as curves.

Let's start off by calculating values of y for which y = 2x over a range of x from 0 to 5. Complete the missing boxes in the table below:

x	0	1	2	3	4	5
y = 2x		2		6		

97

Now, on a sheet of graph paper, draw the x and y axes so as to use as much of the graph paper as possible. Next plot the points for x and y on your graph. You should be able to join them up with a straight line using a ruler.

Question: What is the gradient of the straight line that you have drawn? Hint: use your knowledge of how to measure the gradient of a hill. The diagram below might help.

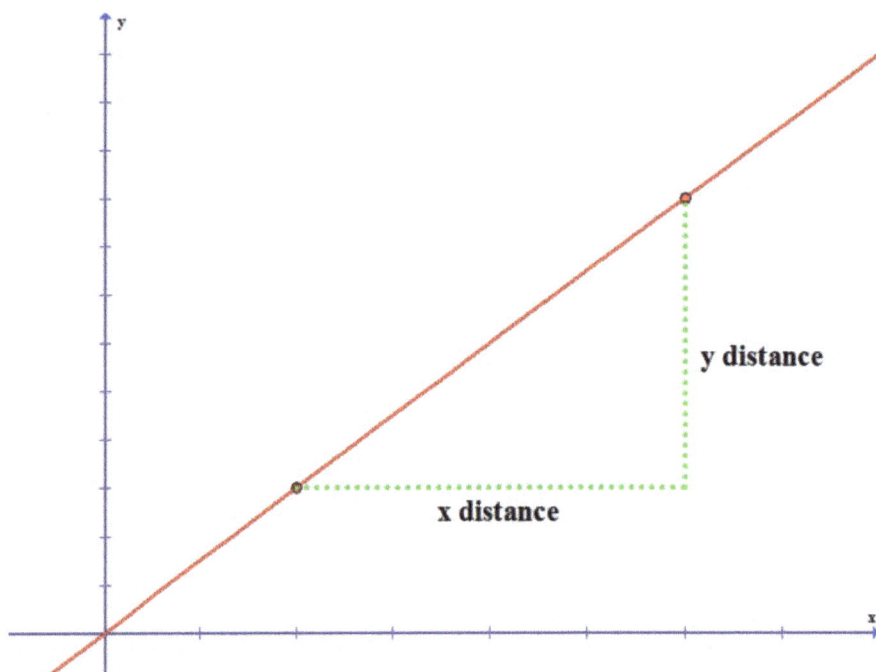

Question: What link is there between the gradient and the equation for y?

So how do we measure the gradient of a curve? We have seen that the gradient of e^x varies along the curve (although it is always equal to e^x) and we can see this when we look at the graph. It starts off nearly flat (gradient nearly 0) and gradually gets steeper so that when x=5 the gradient is e^5 = 148 (approx).

The gradient of a curve of at any point is the gradient of the tangent to the curve drawn at that point.

Let's illustrate this with a typical example (the curve is NOT $y = e^x$):

For the curve shown below, we wish to estimate the gradient of the curve at x = 2, so we start off by marking a point on the curve at x = 2 and then draw a tangent to the curve at this point.

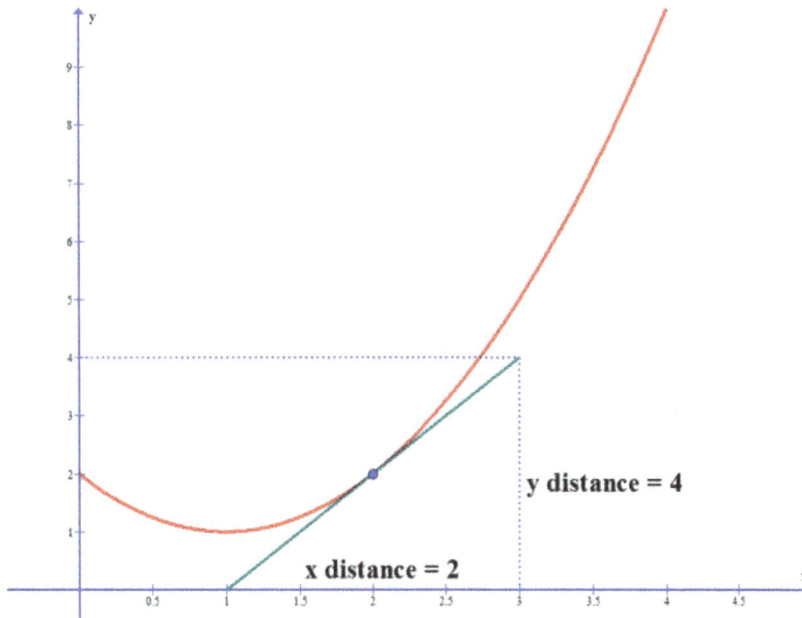

y distance = 4

x distance = 2

Using your tangent, form a convenient triangle, as shown and then measure the corresponding y and x distances. The gradient is, as before:

Gradient = y distance ÷ x distance = 4/2 = 2

That wasn't too difficult was it?

Now go back to your graph for $y = e^x$ and measure the slope at the following values of x:

$$x = -1, x = 0, x = 1$$

Calculate the corresponding values of e^x, using a calculator. Are these each equal to your estimation of the gradient at that point?

Hopefully, we have verified that the gradient of $y = e^x$ is e^x at any value of x (or, at least, the values of x that we picked!)

The Negative Exponential Function e^{-x}

Let's leave gradients now, but sticking with the idea of e^x, let's think about the curve: $y = e^{-x}$ and where this occurs naturally in everyday life.

On a sheet of graph paper draw the curve $y = e^{-x}$ between, say x = 0 and x = 5. Again, it might be useful to draw up a table of values before you start. You will need to use an electronic calculator.

Fill in the missing boxes in the table below (round your answers to 2 decimal places):

x	0	1	2	3	4	5
$y = e^{-x}$			0.14			0.01

Now plot the graph, choosing a suitable scale for your axes to use as much of the graph paper as possible. It should look something like:

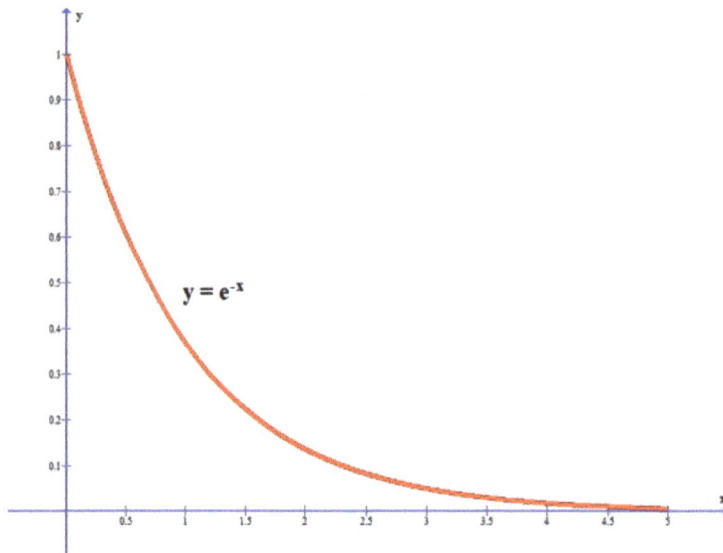

We sometimes refer to this behaviour as *exponential decay*. It occurs naturally e.g. the decay of radioactivity, atmospheric pressure decrease with height, heat transfer, electrical charges and so on.

The Beautiful Equation

Known as Euler's identity the expression: $e^{i\pi} = -1$ is generally admired as a beautiful example of mathematics. It brings together two natural constants, e and π, with i as the square root of -1.

The proof is fairly straightforward, but requires the use of some trigonometric functions.

FURTHER QUESTIONS

1. Another way of calculating the value of e was presented by Harlan Brothers in 2004:

   e = 2/1! + 4/3! + 6/5! + 8/7! + 10/9! + 12/11! + ...

   By calculating the first five terms (up to the 10/9!), how does it compare to the method given at the beginning of this chapter?

2. The value of e can also be estimated using $(1 + n)^{1/n}$ for small values of n. If the estimation gets more accurate as n gets smaller, why can't we just put n=0?

3. Use a scientific calculator (or log tables) to find the common logarithms of 5 and 7. Hence find the value of 5 x 7. Hint: the antilogarithm can be found using the 10^x button.

4. Use a calculator to verify that log (2^5) = 5 log 2. Does this generalise?

5. By using 3 trapeziums then 6, estimate the area under the curve y = x^3 between x = 0 and x=2. Can you say anything about the accuracy of your answer?

6. What is the gradient of the straight line y = 5x + 3?

7. What is the gradient of the curve y = e^x - 3 at x = 2? What about y = $2e^x$ - 3?

8. A negative exponent indicates a reciprocal e.g. 5^{-2} = $1/5^2$. By calculating a few values of x, verify that e^{-x} = $1/e^x$.

9. The age of historical remains can be estimated by a technique called radiocarbon dating. Living organisms such as animals, plants and humans absorb an amount of radioactive carbon-14, and this amount remains constant while they are alive. However, when they die, the carbon-14 level decays and is replaced by nitrogen. This decay follows a negative exponential path whereby the level reduces by a half every 5,730 years. The age of a fossil can be calculated from -5730 ln(p)/0.693 where p is the proportion of carbon-14 remaining relative to a living organism. If the amount remaining is a fifth of the original (i.e. p = 0.2), how old is the fossil?

10. We have met the beautiful equation $e^{i\pi}$ = -1. Can you use Euler's formula: e^x = cos(x) + i.sin(x) to prove this? Note that x is measured in radians as opposed to degrees. Note also that 2π radians = 360 degrees.

Answers to Questions for Chapter Seven

Logarithms

$\log_{10}(6) = 0.7781$ (see the exponents in the example for 2 x 3)
$\ln(3) = 1.0986$ (see exponents in the example for 2 x 3 using base e)

The curve y=1/x

Calculating the area of the three trapeziums:
From your table (and your graph):

x	1	1.5	2	2.5
y = 1/x	1	0.667	0.5	0.4
Area	0.417	0.292	0.225	

In each case the x distance is 0.5

For the first trapezium $y_1 = 1$ and $y_2 = 0.667$ so $(y_1 + y_2)/2 = 1.667/2 = 0.833$
and the area $= x(y_1 + y_2)/2 = 0.5(0.833) = 0.416$ square units

For the second trapezium $y_1 = 0.667$ and $y_2 = 0.5$ so $(y_1 + y_2)/2 = 1.167/2 = 0.583$
and the area $= x(y_1 + y_2)/2 = 0.5(0.583) = 0.291$ square units

For the third trapezium $y_1 = 0.5$ and $y_2 = 0.4$ so $(y_1 + y_2)/2 = 0.9/2 = 0.45$
and the area $= x(y_1 + y_2)/2 = 0.5(0.45) = 0.225$ square units

Adding the three areas together, we get $0.416 + 0.291 + 0.225 = 0.932$ square units
Notice the slight difference between this and the value calculated in the text because I rounded down in these calculations.

Gradients

The gradient of the hill is vertical height ÷ horizontal distance = 100/400 = ¼ = 0.25 (or 25%)

Table for y = 2x

x	0	1	2	3	4	5
y = 2x	0	2	4	6	8	10

The gradient is 2.

A straight line is represented by an equation of the form $y = mx + c$ where m is the gradient.

The gradient for $y = e^x$ for $x = -1$ is 0.368, for $x = 0$ it is 1 and for $x = 1$ it is 2.718

Negative exponential

x	0	1	2	3	4	5
$y = e^{-x}$	1	0.37	0.14	0.05	0.02	0.01

Answers to Further Questions

1. Using the first 5 terms, we get 2.7182815 (true value = 2.7182818 to 7d.p.) If we use the first 5 terms of the original formula, we get 2.7083333

2. Division by zero is not allowed. We say that $1/n$ tends to infinity as n tends to 0, but we can't work with infinity! However, if you try small values of n you can see the trend: $n = 0.1 \rightarrow 2.5937$ $n = 0.01 \rightarrow 2.7048$ $n = 0.001 \rightarrow 2.7169$

3. $\log 5 = 0.6990$, $\log 7 = 0.8451$, $\log 5 + \log 7 = 1.5441$, $10^{1.5441} = 35$

4. In general, $\log y^n = n.\log y$

5. With 3 trapeziums, the estimated area is 4.44 square units, with 6 trapeziums the estimated area is 4.11 (the true area is 4.0 square units). By looking at our two estimates, we can only claim an accuracy of 0 d.p.

6. The gradient is 5. In general, a straight line has the form $y = m.x + c$ where m is the gradient and c is the intercept (where it cuts the y axis).

7. The gradient at x=2 is $e^2 = 7.389$ and for $y = 2e^x - 3$ it is $2e^2 = 14.778$ at $x = 2$.

8. Example: $e^{-3} = 0.0498$, $e^3 = 20.0855$, $1/20.0855 = 0.0498$

9. Age $= -5730 \ln(0.2)/0.693 = -5730 \times (-1.6094) / 0.693 = 13, 307$ years

10. $e^{-\pi} = \cos(\pi) + i.\sin(\pi) = -1 + i0 = -1$

Chapter 8   Maps, Travel, Grid References, Longitude and Latitude

A bear hunter leaves his tent one morning and travels due South for 5 miles. Having not spotted any bears on his path, he decides to travel due East, but after a further 5 miles without seeing any bears, he decides to travel due North. 5 miles on, he sees a tent which he recognises to be the very tent that he had left earlier that day. He is about to enter the tent when a bear springs out, grabs his gun and chases him away. What colour was the bear?

This is one of those classic problems that is so well known that you may have already come across it, but it's a good starting point for our topics in this chapter. This puzzle requires us to spot that the only way he can arrive back at the point where he started by following those directions is that his tent must be at the North Pole. We then need the further information that Polar bears are white and they are only found at the North Pole.

Despite the unlikelihood of a hunter camping at the North Pole, this little puzzle raises some interesting points. First of all, how do you draw a map of the hunter's path on a flat sheet of paper? He travels 5 miles, turns 90° left, travels another 5 miles, turns 90° left again and then travels a further 5 miles. At each stage, he is walking in a straight line, so our diagram would look like:

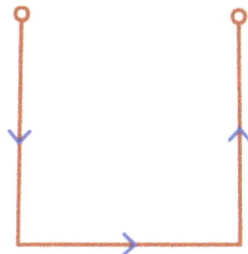

But, this is not the case because we our actually working on the surface of a sphere (although the earth is actually a slightly flattened sphere) and our normal rules of geometry don't seem to work any more. For example, the lines of longitude that resemble the lines on the outside of a peeled orange are parallel 'straight' lines at the equator but they all meet at the poles. Yet, conventional geometry tells us that parallel straight lines cannot meet.

Non-Euclidean Geometry

Out normal geometry is referred to as 'Euclidean Geometry' and is very useful for every-day work. We learn, for instance, that the three internal angles in any triangle add up to 180° and that the area of a circle is πr^2. So here are a couple of things for you to try - if you can get hold of a tennis ball or something similar, it will help. You will also need a basic geometry set that includes a pair of compasses and a protractor.

First, try drawing an equilateral triangle on the surface of the ball. You can use a pair of compasses for this - as long as you are not drawing on a balloon! First use a pen to mark a point on the ball. Then set the distance of the compasses to the side length of your triangle and draw an arc from your marked point. Choose a point on this arc and mark it as shown:

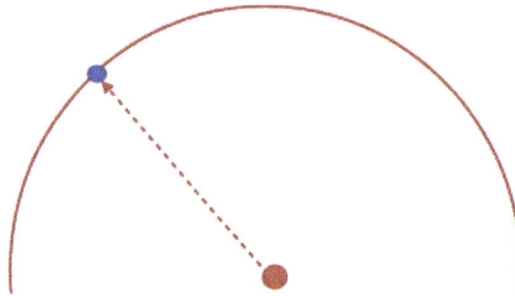

Now put the point of your compasses on the mark on the arc and then draw another arc that crosses your first one:

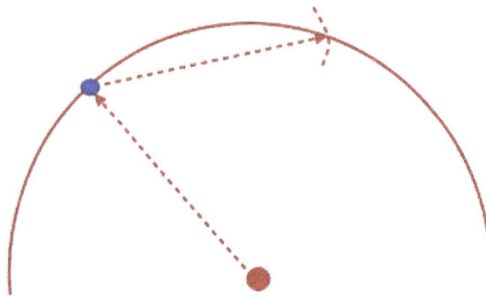

Mark a point where the new arc crosses the old one. You can now draw an equilateral triangle by joining up the three points:

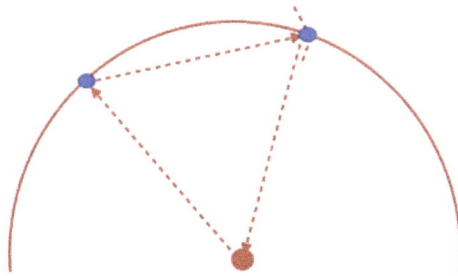

With its three equal sides, it should have three equal internal angles of 60° adding to 180 degrees. Try using a protractor to measure the angles in your triangle - what do you find?

It is possible to draw an equilateral triangle on the surface of a sphere in which all the internal angles are 90 degrees - can you work out how to do it?

Here's another exercise. Use your compasses to draw a circle on the surface of the ball, making it as large as possible. Draw a straight line through the centre using a flexible item with a straight edge and then measure the diameter of your circle. Then, without adjusting your compasses from when you drew the circle, measure the distance between point and pencil to get the radius and double it for the diameter. This measurement of the diameter should be different to the first measure - why is this?

What is the largest circle that you could draw with a pair of compasses on the surface of a sphere?

If I have a ball with a diameter of 10cm, calculate its surface area, given the formula:

$$\text{Surface Area} = 4\pi r^2$$

It is possible to calculate the area of a triangle and other shapes on the surface of a sphere, but such calculations are beyond the scope of this little book!

The term **geodesic** (or *geodetic* as an adjective) is used to describe the shortest distance on a surface between two points lines on a surface. If we are surveying land and taking into account the curvature of the earth, we refer to it as 'geodetic surveying'.

The study of spherical geometry can be traced back to Theodosius of Bithynia, a Greek astronomer and mathematician, at around 100 BC. However, significant developments were made by our old friend Leonhard Euler who wrote a number of papers on the subject in the late 18th century.

Points of the Compass

The magnetic compass has been used for hundreds of years as a navigational aid, particularly at sea. The needle of the compass points to magnetic North and the compass also shows the other so-called cardinal points of East, South and West. Most compasses also show the inter-cardinal (otherwise known as *ordinal*) points of Northeast, Southeast, Southwest and Northwest.

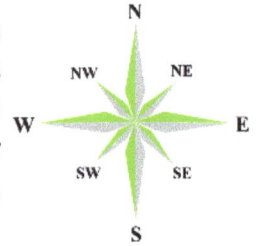

You can make a simple compass by suspending a bar magnet on a piece of string; as long as it is free to rotate, it will align in a North-South direction. If you haven't got a bar magnet, you can use a sewing needle and magnetise it by rubbing it on a piece of silk in the same direction many times. Find a small leaf, put the magnetised needle on the leaf and float the leaf on water.

Magnetic Variation

So why does a magnet point to North? It is because our planet earth has a core that contains molten metal that is magnetised by the rotation of the earth. This results in the equivalent of a giant bar magnet in the centre of the earth from North to South. Unfortunately, this doesn't exactly correspond with the established positions of the North and South poles! The problem is that the earth's magnetic core is not fixed - in fact, it completely reverses roughly every million years! This means that we have a difference between true North and magnetic North which is slowly, but continually changing.

The (true) North and South poles are determined by imagining the earth rotating about a long line going through its centre. Apart from true North and magnetic North, we also have grid North. Although most maps are based upon true North being directly upwards, they are part of a much larger grid system (see later in this chapter) so the vertical grid lines don't quite match up with true North. The Ordnance Survey give a point on each of their maps from which true North and magnetic North are specified. They also indicate the rate of magnetic variation per year. You will need to know these details if you are trying to travel from one place to another following a compass bearing.

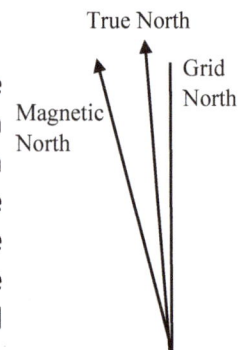

Imagine that you are standing by some landmark (e.g. a bridge across a river) in a remote location. You look at your map and identify your location on the map from the landmark. Further study of the map shows that your destination is 15 km in a direction of 30 degrees, north of your current location. You walk on this course for 15 km, closely keeping to the compass bearing, but you do not find your desired destination - what has gone wrong?

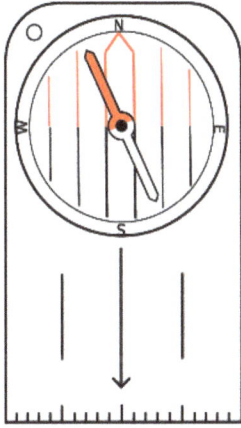

Another name for magnetic variation is *declination* and the Ordnance Survey defines this as *'the horizontal angular difference between true North and magnetic North'*. One problem is that correcting for magnetic variation depends upon where we are - if we travel along the equator we must find a point at which magnetic North and true North are the same. But elsewhere, we must allow for the magnetic variation. This means that when we look at any map, we need to know the magnetic variation based upon some point on that map. But as we move away from this point, we get different values for the angle of correction. Fortunately, the map makers (or O.S. and some others) give us this information for every map that they provide and so we can adjust our compass bearing to put us on course.

What difference does the magnetic variation make in reality? Well, let's go back to our example where we are travelling 15 km and let's suppose the starting point is near the Suffolk coast. We can pinpoint our starting position on our Ordnance Survey (OS) map and we see that our destination is 15 km north of us, according to the grid lines. The map tells us that magnetic north is estimated at 4° west of grid north (it also tells us how we can update this to take into account the annual change since the date on the map, but let's assume that our map is up to date).

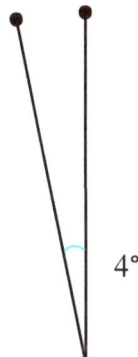

It can be shown (see answers) that if we just followed a course of magnetic north, we would end up about 1.05 km away from our required destination.

If we have a map and a compass, we can find out exactly where we by using a technique known as **resectioning** as long as we can see two or more distinctive landmarks at some distance from each other. This will also involve allowing for magnetic variation. The process is as follows:

Select one of the distinctive landmarks and use your compass to find its bearing.
Use your compass to determine the exact magnetic direction from your location to the feature you chose. Suppose, for example, this bearing is 40° as shown:

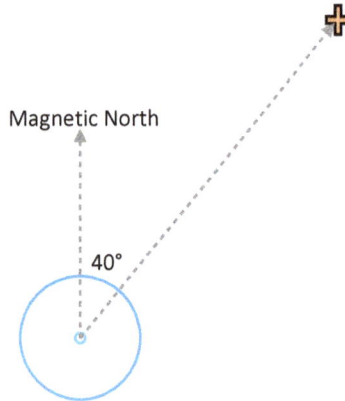

Now adjust for the magnetic variation, so that your bearing is based upon grid north. Let's suppose that magnetic north is 4° west of grid north, so our grid bearing becomes 36°.

Now you need a protractor to measure an angle on your map.

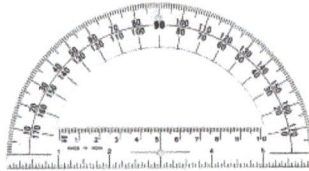

Find your distinctive landmark on your map and use your protractor to find the angle in the reverse direction to your grid bearing. This will be your bearing plus 180° as shown:

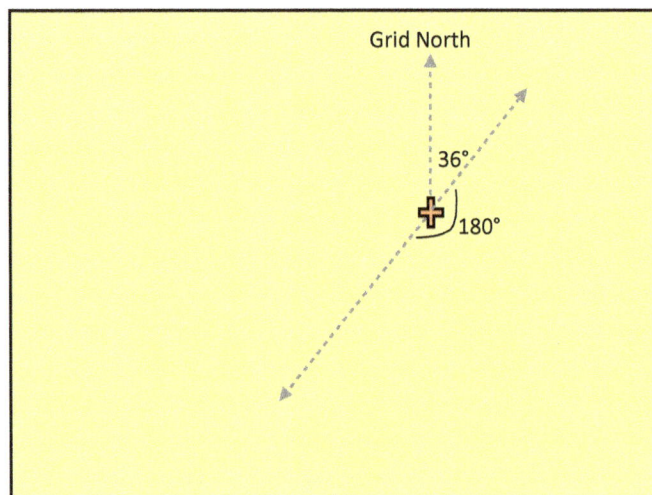

Draw a straight line on your map from the landmark in this reverse direction. Your location will be somewhere along this line.

Repeat the process with a second landmark. Where the two lines intersect will be your location. If you want to be really sure, repeat the process with a third landmark. If all is well, the three lines should intersect at the same point.

Magnetic Storms, the Solar Wind and Navigation Systems

Although the sun is important to us for heat and light, it also has some strange activities that can cause odd effects back here on earth, despite being 93 million miles away.

A *magnetic storm* is the interaction between charged particles coming from the sun and the earth's magnetic field and it can have serious effects. The most well known effects are the auroras - spectacular light displays at the north and south poles. At the north pole, we have the 'Aurora Borealis' (or the northern lights) and at the south pole, the 'Aurora Australis' or the southern lights. For people in the northern hemisphere, the aurora borealis can be seen from places such as Scotland or Alaska when there are clear skies.

Image courtesy of pixabay

Magnetic storms can be caused by sudden massive ejections of plasma from the surface of the sun. These ejections are known *coronal mass ejections* (CMEs) and have a strong magnetic field. A CME usually takes two or three days to reach the earth but it can arrive in under a day if it follows another recent one. Astronauts in space need extra protection from CMEs and the international space station has a shielded core to provide protective cover for those on board.

Magnetic storms can also be caused by variations in the *solar wind*. A regular stream of charged particles is emitted from the sun and this is known as the solar wind. The solar wind is actually made of two parts: a slow wind and a high speed wind. The interaction between these affect the earth's magnetic field resulting in magnetic storms.

The biggest magnetic storm occurred in 1859 and luckily, we haven't had one of such intensity since. In those days, the world didn't have the electricity grids or complex equipment that we have today. However, in 1989 a smaller magnetic storm caused a power failure in Quebec affecting six million people. Usually the storms cause erratic compass bearings, the auroras mentioned earlier, and changes to the density of the ionosphere (an area in the earth's upper sensitive to radio signals). A magnetic storm can have serious effects on GPS systems because their signals are affected due to changes in the ionosphere with position errors of up to several miles. Other navigation systems can also be affected.

It is thought that honey bees use the earth's magnetic field to navigate. Magnetic storms are believed to confuse the bees when they are some way away from their hives.

Image courtesy of pixabay

Maps of the Globe

When you use an atlas to look at a map of the world what do you see? The problem is: how do we map the surface of a sphere onto a two-dimensional page? For many years, the favoured method was the *Mercator projection.*

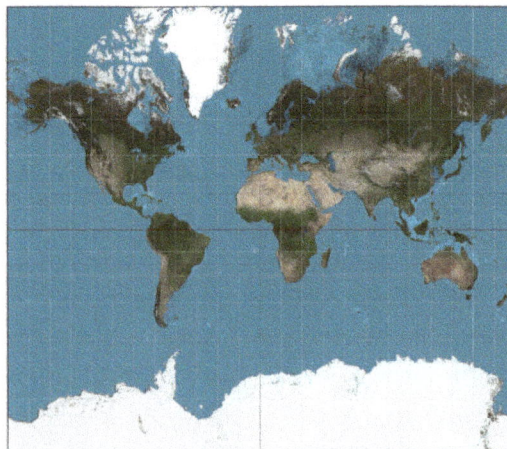

Mercator projection courtesy of Wikimedia Commons

The Mercator projection is an example of a 'cylindrical projection'. Imagine taking a globe and wrapping a large sheet of paper around it so that the paper forms a cylinder and it touches the globe at the equator. Each point on the globe is 'projected' onto the paper.

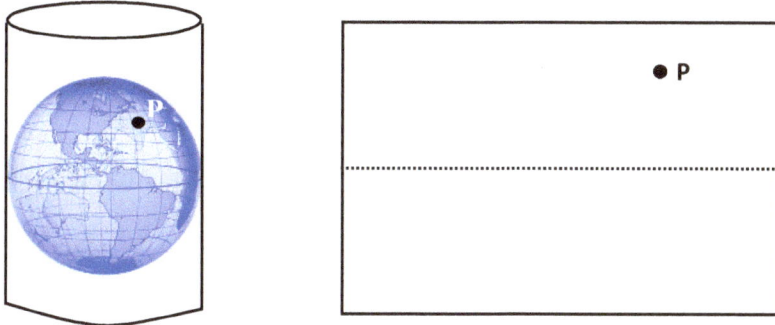

When all the points have been projected, the paper is laid out flat, giving our map of the world. One problem with this method is that distorts land areas the further north or south we move. For example, Greenland appears larger than Australia, even though it is about one third of the area. A popular alternative is the Gall-Peters projection which preserves land areas as shown:

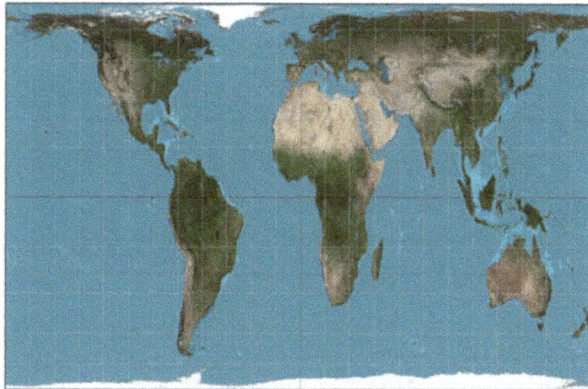

By Strebe (Own work) [CC BY-SA 3.0 (http://creativecommons.org/licenses/by-sa/3.0)], via Wikimedia Commons

Local Area Maps

A map is a drawing that provides visual information about a given location and these have been produced probably as long as man has existed. It enables one person to share their knowledge of an area with another person, making it easier for the other person to find their way.

We have all been fascinated by old stories featuring maps produced by pirates showing where their treasure has been buried.

Modern maps contain a wealth of information showing not only features like roads, buildings, rivers etc. but also information about land height and steepness of slopes. Probably the best maps in the UK are the famous Ordnance Survey (OS) maps which are widely used by walkers, cyclists, climbers and the general public. Although computerised maps are readily available, they rarely show the detail provided by OS maps. If you don't have an OS map at home, most local libraries have a set of them and they are generally available for borrowing. Try to get hold of one before you read the following section - it's not strictly necessary but it will be interesting for you and help your understanding.

Let's start off with some basic facts using OS maps for reference.

One important piece of information about a map is its scale which tells you how the distance on the map relates to the actual distance on the land. It is given as a ratio such as 1:25000 which means that 1cm on the maps represents 25,000 cm on the land (250 m). Note that this is the straight line distance - the actual distance could be a lot more if you are in a mountainous area. Typical OS maps are 1:50000 (Landranger Series), but if you want really good detail of an area, the 1:25000 (Explorer) maps are really useful. Old maps used to be on a scale of 1 inch to the mile, usually written as 1:63360

Maps are divided into a number of squares that form a grid. We have already seen that the vertical grid lines run from north to south and that there is a difference between grid north and magnetic north. Also, there may be a difference between grid north and true north.

Most maps have a **key** or **legend** which is a box that tells you what the symbols on the map mean as well as other information such as the date when the map was produced and magnetic variation. On the OS maps, the key is found in a panel on the right hand side of the map.

Numbering and Naming of Grid Lines

Any location in Great Britain is uniquely identified by its Ordnance Survey (OS) map reference that is based upon a standard known as the British Grid Reference System. Note that this does not extend to Ireland and Northern Ireland, but a similar standard applies there as well.

114

We start off by dividing an area that includes Great Britain into a 5x5 grid of squares whose sides are 500 km in length. These 25 squares are given the letters A-Z (ignoring I).There are four of these squares that cover Great Britain, they have the labels H, N, S, and T.

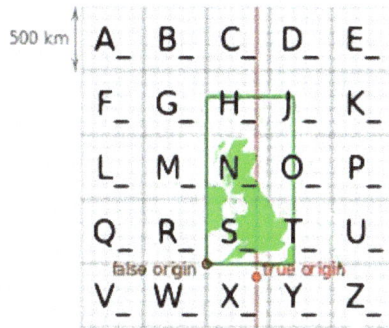

You can see that Great Britain is actually covered by the N, S and T 500 km squares. Note that a 500 kilometre square is not the same as 500 square kilometres!

Each of these squares is also divided up into a 5x5 grid and given a label from A to Z, again ignoring I.

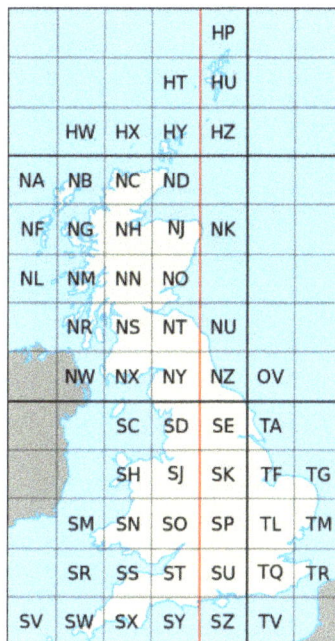

Question: what is the side length of these smaller squares? What is the area of each of these squares?

Question: name the squares that contain (i) Land's End, (ii) The Isle of Anglesey, (iii) The Isle of Skye

So, for Great Britain we can identify each of the 'small' squares by two letters: H, N, S, T followed by one of A, B, C ...... Z (excluding I).

Right, so now we've divided the country into 100km squares, each with a two-letter identifier. But that doesn't pinpoint things very much! For example, London whose area is roughly 1500 square km is in square TQ which has an area of 100 x 100 = 10,000 square km.

The obvious thing to do is to take each of our 100km squares and divide it into 100 smaller squares, so each square is now a 10 x 10 grid of squares.

Question: what is the side length and area of each square in the grid?

This time, we use numbers to identify each line on the grid starting with 0 in the bottom left hand corner and going up in steps of 10. For further accuracy, we go on to divide each of these squares into a 10 x 10 grid, numbering the lines from 0 to 9.

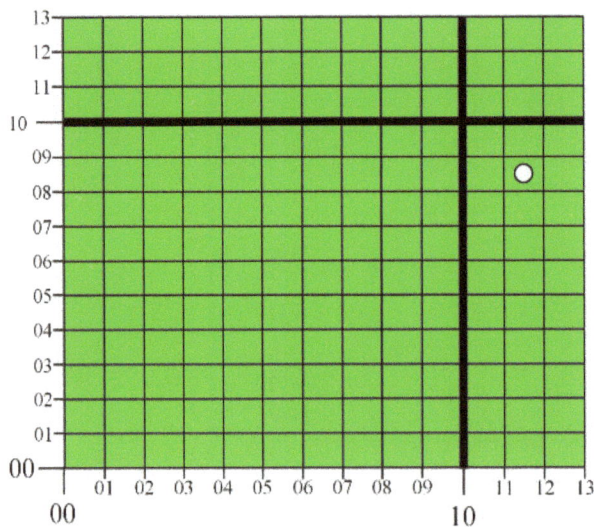

Question: what is the side length and area of each of the smallest squares?

Specifying a Position by its Grid Reference

If you look back at the grid, you'll find one square with a white circle in it. How can I specify this particular square using the numbers available? Just as we specify a point on a graph, we give its x coordinate (in map terms, we call this **eastings**) and then its y coordinate (**northings**). For the spot above, the square would be identified by eastings of 11 and northings of 08. We would normally write these together as 11 08.

116

Now, of course, this same numbering system has been applied to each of the 100 km squares, so we would normally need to add the letters to specify which main square we are referring to. For example, if our grid reference came from square SP, then we would state our reference as SP 11 08.

You have already found that the side length of each of the smaller squares is 1km, so we might still want to be a bit more accurate if we wanted to identify a particular landmark. We can imagine that each smaller square is itself divided up into a 10 x 10 grid, so using our example above, the centre of the white circle is midway or 5 tenths of a square in both the eastings and northings. Our more accurate reference would therefore be SP 115 085 (you can omit the spaces if you wish).

Now suppose our main square was SK then our reference of 115 085 is in a different area of the country. In fact, SK 115 085 would pinpoint a location in the town of Lichfield. It's quite fun to use a website such as www.gridreferencefinder.com to enter a grid reference and see where it is on a map. You can even enter a postcode and get its corresponding grid reference - you may find that they use more numbers to indicate further sub-divisions of each square.

Question: how accurate is a 6-figure map reference using this system?
Note that OS maps also include references to latitude and longitude, although these are not as useful for everyday mapwork. We shall cover these at the end of this chapter.

Navigation on foot

If you're walking in the countryside, an OS map is invaluable. It not only indicates footpaths, rivers and bridges, but includes lots of useful navigational aids in the form of symbols that include electricity pylons, chimneys, towers and masts. Woods are also shown along with their type e.g. coniferous, non-coniferous, coppice, and orchard. O.S. maps contain an incredible amount of information; have a look at the right hand side of any O.S. map for a key to all the symbols and general information.

An Ordnance Survey map doesn't just show features on the ground, but it tells you about the height of the land and steepness of slopes so that you can get a 3-D 'picture' of the area. On maps, we use **_contour lines_** to tell us about these details. Contour lines join points of equal height and are usually shown as thin brown lines with the height shown in metres (measured to the nearest metre above sea level). Each contour line joins back on itself in a 'circular' fashion.

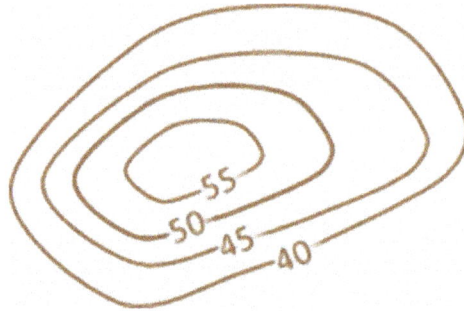

Drawing a Cross-Section

Suppose you have decided to take a walk over some open country in a straight line for, say, 5km. You look at your OS map and see that there are some hills involved and you think it would be nice to have some sort of picture of the route in advance. One option is to draw a cross section of the route, as if you were looking at a sideways slice of the earth along this route, for example:

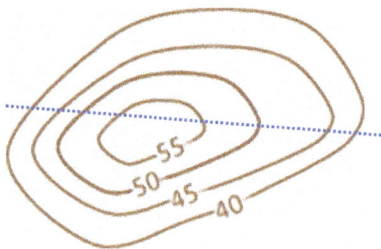

Distance	Height
3	40
7	45
11	50
16	55
26	55
35	50
45	45
48	40

We start by drawing a line on the map showing our intended route. Then, measure the distance from the starting point to each point where the line crosses a contour line. Draw up a table, as shown above, with these distances and the height of the points. From this, you can draw the cross-section.

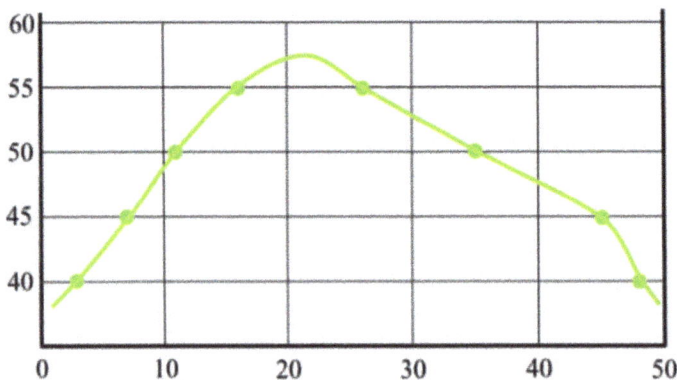

118

Try one for yourself, using the simple diagram below.

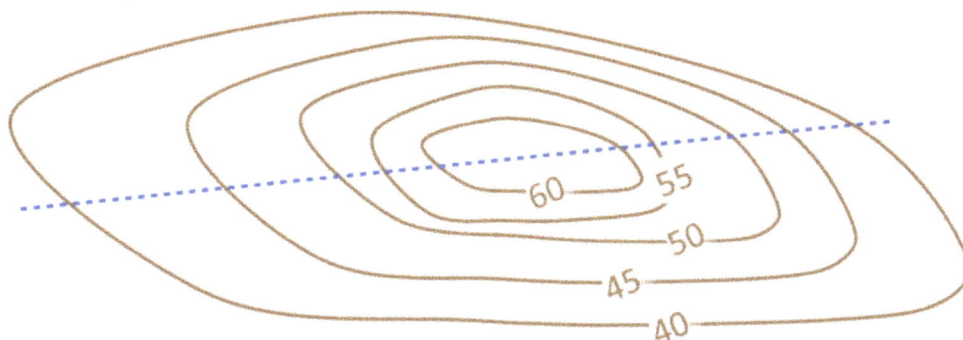

You may have spotted that a hill is steepest when the contour lines are close together, so this is worth knowing when planning a walk.

You will find similar lines to contour lines in other settings e.g. weather maps often show lines called *isobars* which join points of equal atmospheric pressure. You might also find *isotherms* which are lines joining points of equal temperature. Can you find any other examples? Some maps such as those indicating ocean temperatures use different colours between the contours to give an instant visual impression.

When is a Mile not a Mile?

In many parts of the world, distance is measured in *metres* and when travelling, a convenient unit is the *kilometre*. However, in the United Kingdom and America, the *mile* is more commonly used (1 mile = 1.609 km). Other countries that still use the mile are Liberia and Myanmar (also known as Burma).

The mile originated in ancient Rome where the Roman soldiers used a measure of a thousand paces (pairs of steps) to mark their progress when marching. Unfortunately, this didn't always measure the same distance and the emperor Agrippa is thought to have used his own foot to create a standard Roman foot in 29 BC. A pace was officially set at 5 Roman feet and the mile became 5,000 Roman feet (roughly 0.92 of our normal miles).

The English statute mile (to give it a formal name) was established in 1593 during the reign of Queen Elizabeth I, but had its origins in the Roman mile. It is divided into 1,760 yards and each yard is 3 feet in length. With 12 inches in a foot, we get 63,360 inches to a mile.

The international mile, equal to the English statute mile, was established in 1959 and was accepted in countries such as the USA, Canada, and Australia. By this time, other parts of the United Kingdom had long since abandoned the Welsh mile (3.84 miles), the Scots mile (1.12 miles) and the Irish mile (1.62 miles). Other countries such as Hungary, Croatia, and Germany had their own miles of different lengths. The United States also uses the US survey mile which is very slightly bigger than an international mile although the difference is so small that the two are usually regarded as equivalent.

So if there are different miles on land, it should not be a surprise that a mile is not a mile when we are at sea! A **nautical mile** is 1.151 miles. If you take a circle of the same size as the earth's equator and form a sector from a central angle of $1/60^{th}$ of a degree (1 *minute*), the length of the arc is 1 nautical mile

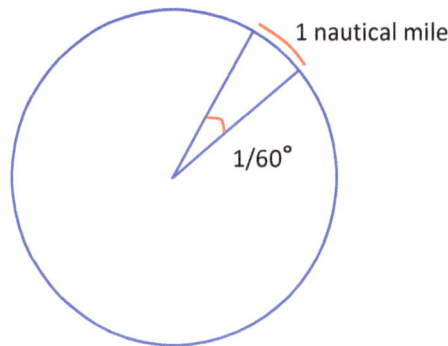

But would it surprise you to learn that there are different nautical miles? Until 1929, the US nautical mile was 2½ inches longer than its UK counterpart (also known as the Admiralty mile). We now have the *international nautical mile* which is about 46 inches shorter than either of them (at exactly 1852 metres). There is also the *sea mile* which means different things to different people and, according to one definition, varies in length according to whereabouts you are on the earth!

Ships measure their speed in knots where 1 knot equals 1 nautical mile per hour. The term *knot* comes from the way that sailors measured their speed in olden days. They would throw a log attached to a long rope, knotted at regular intervals) from the stern of the ship. Using a 30-second sand timer, they counted the number of knots passed out in that 30 second period and converted this into nautical miles per hour.

Although this method was reasonably accurate, it didn't take into account the effect of ocean currents which can speed up or slow down a ship. Modern methods of measuring speed at sea are still called logs and GPS systems which are not affected by currents are a popular choice.

Latitude and Longitude

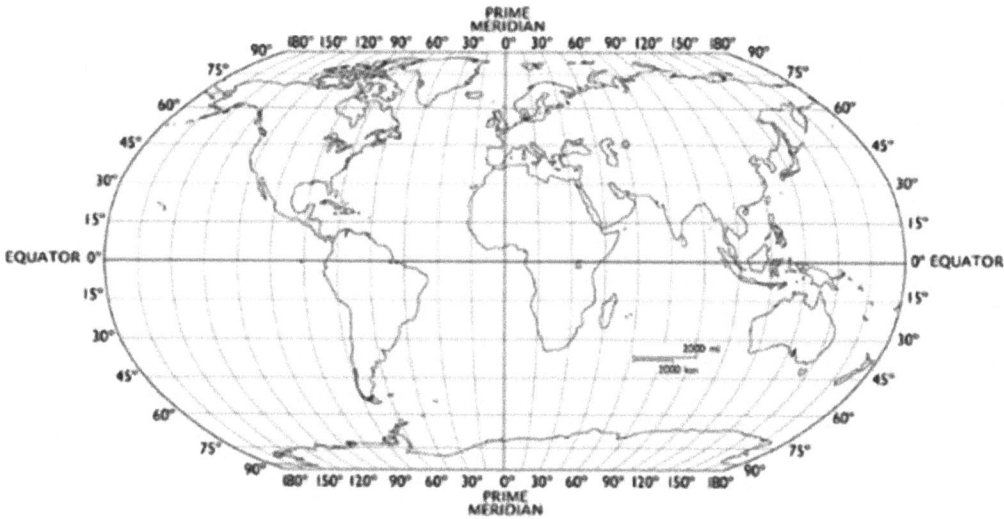

Image courtesy of worldatlas.com

We began this chapter with a reference to non-Euclidean geometry and mentioned lines of longitude as an example of where parallel lines could cross. The lines of longitude are the vertical lines shown above and these are also called *meridians*. They are numbered in degrees east and west of the *prime meridian* of 0 degrees that passes through Greenwich in England. They meet at 180° east and west in the Pacific Ocean which is know as the *international date line*.

The horizontal lines are known as the *lines of latitude* (also called *parallels*) and are north and south of 0° at the equator. They extend from 90° north to 90° south.

The lines of latitude and longitude enable us to locate any place on earth. But by themselves, they are a bit too far apart to be very accurate, so we subdivide each degree into 60 minutes and each minute into 60 seconds. Each degree of latitude represents a distance of about 69 miles and each degree of longitude is also about 69 miles at the equator.

As an example, the Royal Shakespeare Theatre in Stratford Upon Avon is at latitude 52 degrees, 11 minutes, 21 seconds (written 52° 11' 21") and longitude -1° 42' 25". It is quite common to express the minutes and seconds as a decimal e.g. 52.189180, -1.706930. Note that negative values mean south of the equator, or west of the prime meridian.

Websites such as iTouchMap.com allow you to find the latitude and longitude from a point on a map or other information such as a postcode.

FURTHER QUESTIONS

1. If a map has a scale of 1:50000, what does a distance of 2.5 cm on the map represent?

2. How accurately can we specify a location in terms of latitude and longitude if the location is on the equator?

3. Draw a cross section of the route shown on the following map:

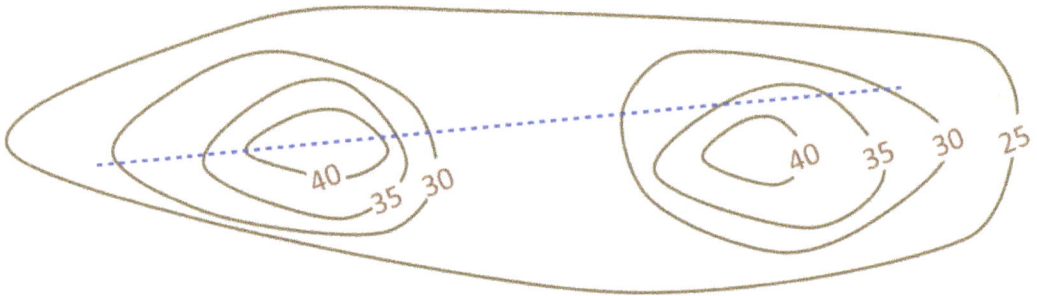

4. A ship is travelling at 10 knots. What is its speed in miles per hour?

5. The latitude of a given location is stated to be 32.632470 degrees. What is this in degrees, minutes and seconds and which hemisphere is it in?

6. The circumference of the earth is 40,075 km, what is its radius?

7. If you could form a loop of cord around the equator and extended its length by 1 metre, what distance would it now be from the earth? Assume that the loop is equidistant from the earth's surface throughout. If you did the same with a CD of radius 6 cm, what would be the distance?

8. If the earth were perfectly round, what would its surface area be?

9. The distance between knots on a log line was 14.4 metres. If 20 knots passed out over the 30 second period of the sand glass, at what speed was the ship travelling. Give your answer in knots.

10. If you were standing at the magnetic north pole, where would your compass point?

Answers to Questions for Chapter Eight

Equilateral triangle on the surface of a sphere:
Imagine drawing on the earth. Start at the north pole and draw a line down to the equator. From here draw a line at 90° to the first i.e. along the equator for a quarter of length of the equator. Now draw another line at 90° to the equator, back to the north pole. Result: an equilateral triangle in which the internal angles are each 90°.

Different measurements of diameter: your compasses measure the straight line distance which is shorter than the length of arc.

Largest circle with compasses:

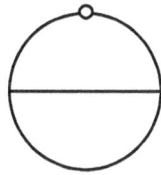

Surface Area = $4\pi r^2$ = 4 x 3.142 x 5^2 = 314.2 square cm.

OS Maps: subdividing a 500 km square into a 5 x 5 grid gives 100 km squares, each with an area of 10,000 sq. km.

i) Land's End is in SW (ii) Anglesey is in SH   (iii) Skye is in NG

Dividing the 100 km squares results in a 10 x 10 grid of squares each with side length 10 km and area 100 sq. km.

Further subdivision: side = 1 km, area = 1 sq. km.

Accuracy of 6 figure map reference: Each 1 km square is represented by a 10 x 10 grid, so each smaller square has side length 100 m and thought of as having an internal 10 x 10 grid of side width 10 m. Therefore any point is specified to an accuracy of + or - 5 m.

Answers to Further Questions

1. 2.5 cm x 50,000 = 125,000 cm = 1250 m = 1.25 km

2. Smallest distance that can be specified in this way is 1 second (1") of arc. Taking a degree of longitude to be 69 miles at the equator, one second would represent 69/3600 miles i.e. 0.0192 miles or about 34 yards or 31 metres. So, if we specify a location to the nearest minute are accuracy is + or - 17 yards.

3.

Distance	0	3	15	21	39	41	46	72	84	101	109	111
Height	?	30	35	40	40	35	30	30	35	35	30	?

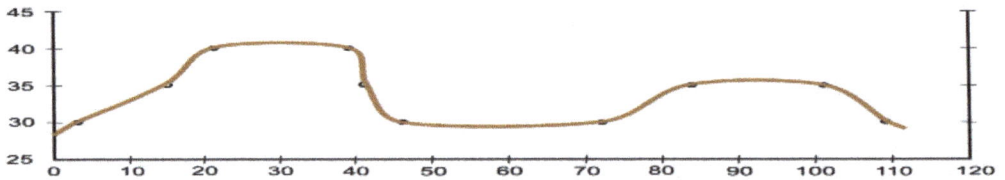

Note that it is possible to estimate the height at 0 and 111 by assuming a steady slope between the contour lines e.g. height at 0 = 25 + 5/8 of 5 = 28 (approximately)

4. 10 knots = 10 x 1.151 = 11.51 miles per hour

5. Find the number of minutes: 0.63247 x 60 = 37. 9482 giving 37 minutes
   Find the number of seconds: 0.9482 x 60 = 56.892 giving 57 seconds (rounded)
   So, 33.632470° = 33° 37′ 57″

6. 40,075 = 2πR so R = 40,075 ÷ (2π) = 6,378 km (although the mean radius of 6,371 km is usually quoted).

7. 16 cm in both cases!

8. Surface Area = $4\pi R^2$ and using R = 6,378 km, we get 511,185,932 sq. km. (of which, about 70% is ocean)

9. Distance moved in 30 seconds = 20 x 14.4 = 288 metres

   Speed = 288 x 2 x 60 = 34,560 metres/ hour or 21.47 miles per hour or 18.65 knots

10. If you were holding your compass perfectly horizontally, it wouldn't point in any particular direction.

Chapter 9   Mathematical Tricks

One of the penalties of being a mathematician is that everyone expects you to be fast in calculating things involving everyday numbers such as shares of a restaurant bill. In reality, many mathematicians are hopeless with numbers because arithmetical ability is not greatly important when compared to competence in the many and varied branches of mathematics. For example, if we want to define the area of a circle in relation to its radius, it would be difficult to do this without the formula $A = \pi.r^2$, and so most mathematicians deal with letters rather than numbers to express their ideas and rules.

However, a good mathematician should have a few tricks up the sleeve to impress friends or to estimate calculations. Never trust an electronic calculator - they don't make mistakes, but you do! Anyway, let's have a look at a few useful tricks.

Subtraction Tricks

Subtraction by Rounding

We often need to do subtraction in our head e.g. when working out the change we should receive when paying for something, or scoring in a game of darts. This method can be quite useful in those situations.

As a simple example, consider 63 - 37. The trick is to round up the second number, in this case 37 gets rounded up to 40 by adding 3. Now do 63 - 40 = 23 and add the remaining 3 to get the correct answer 26.

Try another one: 892 - 276. There are various possibilities here. One was is to round the 276 up to 300 by adding 24. Then 892 - 300 = 592, so the result is 592 + 24 = 616. But could we have made the process a bit easier? We might spot that if we added 16 to 276, we get 292. Now we can do 892 -292 = 600 then add 16, giving 616, as before. It's all a question of spotting the route that is simplest for you.

Try doing the following subtractions using this method: 487 - 299, 939 - 456, 1084 - 737

Subtraction by Complement

Complement (as opposed to *compliment*) means *'that which completes or fills up'* - according to Chambers Dictionary. So if, for example, we had a 1-litre bottle containing 70 centilitres of water, the amount required to fill the bottle would be the complement of this amount i.e. 30 centilitres.

For numbers, we talk about things like the 9s complement which involves the amount required to 'top up' a given number to make every digit a 9. For example the 9s complement of 157 would be 842.

Now the trick for subtraction is form the 9s complement of the number to be subtracted and add it to the other number. Add another 1 for good measure, throw away the first digit of the result and that's your answer!

For example: 475 - 157 (the first number is called the *minuend* and the second, the *subtrahend*)

	475
+	842 (the 9s complement of 157)
=	1317
+	1
=	1318

And throw away the leading 1 to get the result 318.

If the second number has fewer digits than the first, we need to add leading zeros. For example 1254 - 89

Write 89 as 0089 and form its 9s complement to get 9910

	1254
+	9910
=	11164
+	1
=	11165

Throw away the first 1 to get the result 1165

It is usually simpler to add the 1 to the 9s complement when we form it. The result of adding 1 to the 9s complement is called the **10s complement**.

So how does this trick work? Well, the 10s complement of any number x, is $10^N - x$, where N is the number of digits in each number.

To calculate y - x, we use y + 10s complement of x, giving $y - x + 10^N$ (and the 10^N is discarded).

If the second number is bigger than the first, the result will be negative and the extra digit will not be generated. In this case, we need to form the 10s complement of the result.

For example, 192 - 236. As before, form the 10s complement of 236 which is 763 + 1 = 764

$$
\begin{array}{rl}
 & 192 \\
+ & 764 \\
= & 956 \quad \text{Note that no extra digit has been generated}
\end{array}
$$

The 10s complement of 956 is 043 + 1 = 44, so the result is - 44.

An alternative is to swap the numbers at the outset, so that you are subtracting a smaller number from a larger one and then remember to put a minus sign in front of the result. The technique was used in early mechanical calculating machines and is still used in modern computers where the 2s complement is very easily obtained for binary numbers. We also saw in chapter 6 how easy it is to form logic circuitry to add two binary numbers together.

Try the same subtractions using this method: 487 - 299, 939 - 456, 1084 - 737

Division Tricks

Denominators ending in 9

This is a rather nice trick to convert fractions to decimals where the denominator ends in a 9. It can be quite impressive because, with a little practice, you can reel off the decimal digits without writing anything down!

Let's use 41/69 as an example. This doesn't look like the sort of conversion that you could easily do in your head! We'll start off by writing it down, but you'll soon see how each successive digit can be done without putting pen to paper.

First round up the denominator, so in our example, 69 goes to 70. Then remove the 0 to get 7 which is the number that we shall use in our division and at each stage we note the remainder and write it to the left of our result.

So starting with 41 and dividing by 7, we get 5 remainder 6. We form a new number from these digits by writing the remainder to the left of the result (the _quotient_). This gives us 65, which we again divide by 7 giving 9 remainder 2. Write this as 29 and again divide by 7 as shown:

Divided by 7	41
Remainder	Quotient
6	5
2	9
1	4
0	2
2	0
6	2
6	8
5	9
3	8

Now read off the result from the number column from the second row to get 0.594202898.... If you are doing this without writing anything down, you only have to remember the new number at each stage before doing the division. You then speak out the integer part of the division, while calculating the remainder and forming the next number.

Try using this method to express 15/39 as a decimal.

Division by 7

Not such a great trick as the above, but more of an observation. If we look at simple fractions with 7 as the denominator, we can spot a pattern (the digits in red indicate the starting digits for the next fraction):

$$1/7 = 0.142857 \text{ (repeated)}$$
$$2/7 = 0.285714 \text{ (repeated)}$$
$$3/7 = 0.428571 \text{ (repeated)}$$
$$4/7 = 0.571428 \text{ (repeated)}$$
$$5/7 = 0.714285 \text{ (repeated)}$$
$$6/7 = 0.857142 \text{ (repeated)}$$

So, if you can remember the sequence 142857, it's not too difficult to quote the remaining single-digit fractions. It follows that you could then quote the result for any number divided by 7, because the result will always be the quotient plus the remainder e.g. 22/7 = 3 + 1/7 = 3.142857... (a much used approximation to π).

Multiplication Tricks

The Line Method (Japanese Multiplication Method)

This is a graphical method for multiplying two numbers.

We start with an example that illustrates a multiplication of two 2-digit numbers (this method can be extended to the multiplication of a wider range of numbers).

First consider a typical problem, 23 x 42.

We take each number in turn and draw a number of straight lines for each digit, starting from some reference point (left hand corner), beginning with the most significant digit.

So, our example problem of 23 x 42 would be drawn as follows:

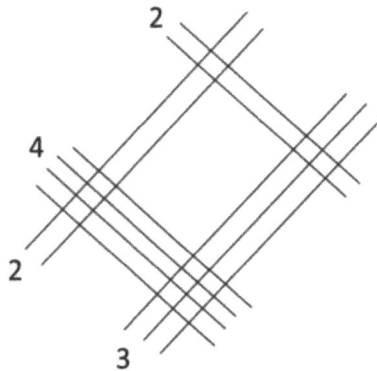

Now, starting from the left and its opposite on the right, isolate regions where the lines intersect. Ignore the middle ground!

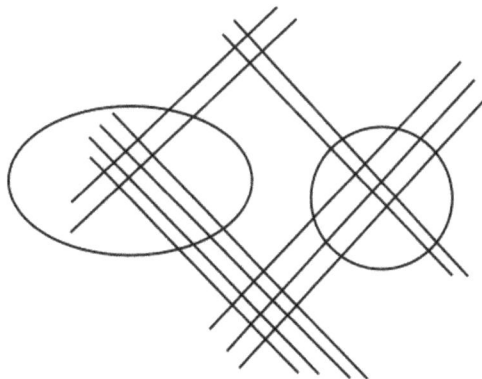

Now count the number of intersections within each region. In our example, we have: left-hand region: 8 intersections, intermediate region: 12 + 4 intersections, and the right-hand region 6 intersections.

Write these values down in the corresponding parts of the diagram:

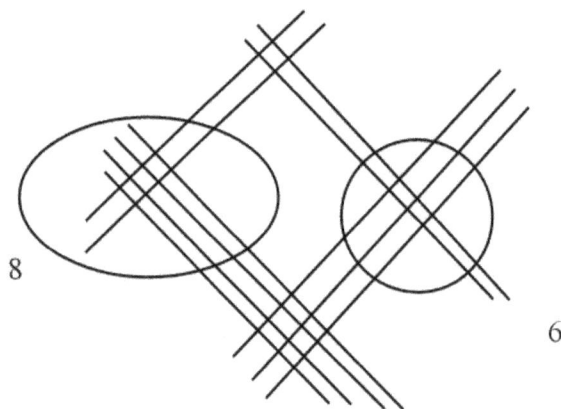

$$12 + 4 = 16$$

Now, starting from the right hand side, we look at the results. If any result contains more than a single digit, we keep the rightmost digit and take the leftmost digit and add it on to the result on its left.

So, in our example, we start from the right and see 6, no problem here, so move left. We come to the result 16, so we keep the 6 but move the 1 leftward where we add it on to that number.

Looking left, we have the result 8 and by adding the 1 from our previous item, we get 9.

Now read the result from left to right to get 966 which is the correct answer for 23 x 42

Exercise: try using this method to calculate 17 x 34.

The Russian Peasant Method

Another interesting multiplication trick is the 'Russian Peasant Method' which involves repeatedly doubling the first number and halving the second, ignoring any remainder.

Consider 19 x 57. We write the two numbers as two columns and proceed as above, crossing out all the even numbers in the right-hand column:

19	57	
38	28	Ignore
76	14	Ignore
152	7	
304	3	
608	1	

Now add up the numbers in the left-hand column that belong to the non-ignored values. 19 + 152 + 304 + 608 = 1083 (the correct result!). You might think about the fact that 57 in binary is 111001 (look at the right hand column from bottom to top) and that 19 x 57 = 19 x (1 + 8 + 16 + 32) = 19 x 1 + 19 x 8 + 19 x 16 + 19 x 32

Exercise: try using this method to calculate 23 x 74

Conversion Tricks

Decimal to Binary

Here are a couple of ways of converting decimal (or denary) numbers into binary. Note that the numbers must be whole numbers, although there are ways of converting a fractional part of a number.

The first method involves repeatedly dividing by 2 and noting the remainder until we get down to 0. Suppose that we want to convert 237 into binary.

237	Rem
118	1
59	0
29	1
14	1
7	0
3	1
1	1
0	1

Now read the result from the remainder column from bottom to top, giving 11101101 which is the binary equivalent of 237.

Here's one for you to try. Convert 139 into binary.

The second method involves writing out the decimal equivalent of each binary digit and working out which bits you have to add in to make up the number. The decimal values of, say, an 10-digit binary number are as shown:

512	256	128	64	32	16	8	4	2	1

So suppose we wanted to convert 175 into binary. We start by comparing our number to the values in the table, working from left to right until we find one that is less than or equal to our value. Put a 1 underneath this value.

512	256	128	64	32	16	8	4	2	1
		1							

Now subtract this value from the number that we are trying to convert. 175 − 128 = 47 and repeat the process with this number. 64 is greater than 47, so we don't want that. Put a 0 underneath that. 32 is less than 47, so put a 1 under that and subtract 32 from 47, leaving 15.

512	256	128	64	32	16	8	4	2	1
		1	0	1					

Repeating this process, we end up with the table below, from which we can read off the result 10101111.

512	256	128	64	32	16	8	4	2	1
		1	0	1	0	1	1	1	1

Converting Between Different Units of Measurement

We often wish to convert between different units, for example miles to kilometres, gallons to litres, and so on. Some of these conversions can be confusing – especially if we can't quite remember the conversion factor, or whether we have to multiply or divide!

There is a systematic approach, attributed to William Stroud, a professor of physics at what is now the University of Leeds in the late nineteenth century. The method is a good one because it can make complicated conversions quite straightforward and allows you to use the facts that you can remember.

132

The basic principle is that if you multiply a value by something equal to one, you don't change its value. This appears in another guise with the idea of 'cancelling' in fractions where we divide top and bottom by the same value. Also remember that if the overall value of a fraction is equal to one, we can turn it upside down if we wish to do so e.g. 1 Kg / 2.2 lb = 2.2 lb / 1 Kg

When we use this method, we write the unit names in at each stage. Let's start off with a simple example. Consider converting 5 gallons into litres and let's suppose that we can only remember that there are 8 pints in one gallon and that 1 litre is equal to 1 ¾ pints. Our calculation will look as shown below (explanations afterwards):

$$5 \text{ gallons} \times \frac{8 \text{ pints}}{1 \text{ gallon}} \times \frac{1 \text{ litre}}{1.75 \text{ pints}} = \frac{40 \text{ litres}}{1.75} = 22.86 \text{ litres}$$

Start with 5 gallons, we multiply it by something equal to one i.e. 8 pints / 1 gallon, choosing the fraction so that the units (in this case gallons) cancel out. We then multiply the result by something else equal to one i.e. 1 litre / 1.75 pints so that the pints will cancel out. This leaves us with the result in litres.

Let's try a more difficult one. Convert 30 miles per hour into kilometres per hour, taking 1 metre to be equal to 39.37 inches.

$$\frac{30 \text{ miles}}{\text{hour}} \times \frac{1760 \text{ yards}}{1 \text{ mile}} \times \frac{3 \text{ feet}}{1 \text{ yard}} \times \frac{12 \text{ inches}}{1 \text{ foot}} \times \frac{1 \text{ metre}}{39.37 \text{ inches}} \times \frac{1 \text{ kilometre}}{1000 \text{ metres}}$$

$$= \frac{30 \times 1760 \times 3 \times 12 \times 1 \times 1 \text{ kilometres}}{1 \times 1 \times 1 \times 39.37 \times 1000 \text{ hour}} = \frac{48.3 \text{ kilometres}}{\text{hour}}$$

Here's one for you to try. What is one ton in metric tonnes? Use 1 ton = 2240 pounds, 1 kilogram = 2.2 pounds and 1 tonne = 1000 kilograms.

Miscellaneous Tricks

Here are a couple of tricks that you can use to impress your friends. The first one was presented by Martin Gardner in his book 'Mathematics, Magic and Mystery' and attributed to Royal V. Heath.

Finding the Sum of a Fibonacci Sequence

Get a friend to think of two small numbers and to generate a 10 number Fibonacci sequence from these (remember that each number in the sequence is obtained by adding the two previous numbers). You ask your friend not to tell you the two numbers and you look away while the sequence is being written down. You then turn round, glance at the sequence and immediately write down the sum of the numbers!

Suppose your friend chooses 2 and 5 as the starting numbers. The sequence is:

| 2 | 5 | 7 | 12 | 19 | 31 | 50 | 81 | 131 | 212 |

You pick out the fourth number from the end of the sequence and multiply it by 11 and this gives the sum of the sequence! In this case we have 50 x 11 = 550. Multiplying by 11 is easy because all we have to do is multiply by 10 and add the original number. However, the trick can go wrong if your friend makes a mistake when generating the sequence!

You might find that multiplying by 10 and adding the original number gets a bit tricky when larger numbers are involved. Let's suppose that your friend has chosen 8 and 9 as the starting values. We then get the sequence:

| 8 | 9 | 17 | 26 | 43 | 69 | 112 | 181 | 293 | 474 |

Now we have to multiply 112 by 11 which, if we do it the standard way involves adding 1120 and 112. OK that's not too bad – the answer is 1232 – but this is perhaps an indication that the mental arithmetic might get tricky when we are under pressure to deliver an immediate answer! Here's another trick that might come in useful here, or one that is impressive on its own.

Multiplication by 11

If we think about the method of multiplying by 10 and then adding the original number, we can find another way of multiply by 11. Consider 112 x 11 as an example:

$$
\begin{array}{ll}
112 \times 10 \quad = & 1\,1\,2\,0 \\
\text{Add } 112 & \underline{1\,1\,2} \\
\text{Result} & 1\,2\,3\,2 \\
\end{array}
$$

Another way of expressing this is as follows:

- Copy the first digit: 1
- Add the first and second digits: 1 + 1 = 2
- Add the second and third digits: 1 + 2 = 3
- Copy the last digit: 2
- Write down the result: 1232

Here's another example, multiply 2436 by 11:

- Copy the first digit: 2
- Add the first and second digits: 2 + 4 = 6
- Add the second and third digits: 4 + 3 = 7
- Add the third and fourth digits: 3 + 6 = 9
- Copy the last digit: 6
- Write down the result: 26796

Now, you might have spotted a possible problem – what happens when we add two digits and the sum is greater than 9? No problem – we simply carry the 1 to the previous digit.

Consider the following example, multiply 3581 by 11:

- Copy the first digit: 3
- Add the first and second digits: 3 + 5 = 8
- Add the second and third digits: 5 + 8 = 13 which becomes 3 and add one to the previous result -> 8 + 1 = 9
- Add the third and fourth digit: 8 + 1 = 9
- Copy the last digit: 1
- Write down the result: 39391

You might prefer to work from right to left. Either way, you can achieve good speed by trying some of your own examples.

FURTHER QUESTIONS

1. Use 'subtraction by rounding' to calculate:

    (i)   265 - 189
    (ii)   729 - 547
    (iii)   846 - 377

2. Use 'subtraction by complement' to calculate:

    (i)   432 - 269
    (ii)   827 - 536
    (iii)   821 - 69

3. (i) What is 6/19 as a decimal?
    (ii) If n is any number between 1 and 9 inclusive, show that $n/9 = 0.nnnnnnn....$

4. Use the Line method to calculate 31 x 24

5. Use the Russian Peasant method to calculate 23 x 49

6. Use 'halving and remainder' to convert 187 into binary

7. Use the table method to convert 729 into binary

8. If petrol costs 108 pence per litre, use the Stroud method to convert this into pounds per gallon. Take 1 gallon = 8 pints, 1 litre = 1.75 pints, and 1 pound = 100 pence.

9. What is the sum of the 10-term Fibonacci sequence 1, 3, 4, 7, 11, 18, 29, 47, 76, 123

10. Calculate 153 x 11 using the quick method in this chapter.

Answers to Questions for Chapter Nine

Subtraction by Rounding
Remember that these can be done in different ways!

487 - 299: 299 + 1 = 300, 487 - 300 = 187, 187 + 1 = 188
939 - 456: 456 + 44 = 500, 939 - 500 = 439, 439 + 44 = 483
1084 - 737: 737 + 3 = 740, 1084 - 740 = 344, 344 + 3 = 347

Subtraction by Complement

487 - 299: 487 + 700 = 1187, 1187 + 1 = 1188, discard leading 1: 188
939 - 456: 939 + 543 = 1482, 1482 + 1 = 1483, discard leading 1: 483
1084 - 0737: 1084 + 9262, 10346, 10346 + 1 = 10347, discard leading 1: 347

Note that in the last case, it would have worked without adding a leading zero, but we couldn't always get away with this e.g. if the subtraction had been 1084 -37 we have:

1084 + 9962 = 11046, leading to the correct answer of 1047 whereas without the leading zeros, we get 1084 + 62 = 1146, leading to the incorrect answer of 147.

Denominators ending in 9: 15/39

Divided by 4	15
Remainder	Quotient
3	3
1	8
2	4
0	6
2	1
1	5
3	3
1	8
2	4

15/39 = 0.384615384.....

Note that we can spot a recurring sequence of numbers (384615)

Line Drawing: 17 x 34

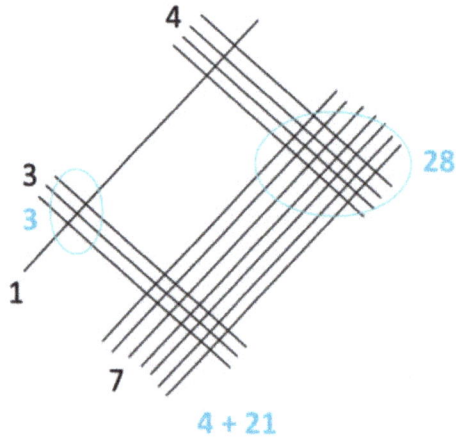

Rightmost digit = 8 and add the 2 to 4 + 21 to get 27. Middle digit is 7 and add the 2 to 3 giving 5 as the leftmost digit. Result 578.

Russian Peasant Method: 23 x 74

23	74	ignore
46	37	
92	18	ignore
184	9	
368	4	ignore
736	2	ignore
1472	1	

Result: 46 + 184 + 1472 = 1702

Decimal to Binary: 139

139	Rem
69	1
34	1
17	0
8	1
4	0
2	0
1	0
0	1

Answer 10001011

Answers to Further Questions

1. Possible approaches are:

    (i)   265 - 189: 189 + 11 = 200,   265 - 200 = 65,   65 + 11 = 76
    (ii)   729 - 547: 547 + 3 = 550,   729 -550 = 179,   179 + 3 = 182
    (lii)   846 - 377: 377 + 23 = 400,   846 - 400 = 446,   446 + 23 = 469

2.
    (i)   432 - 269: 432 + 730 = 1162, 1162 + 1 = 1163 discard leading 1: 163
    (ii)   827 - 536: 827 + 463 = 1290, 1290 + 1 = 1291 discard leading 1: 291
    (lii)   821 - 69:   821 + 930 = 1751, 1751 + 1 = 1752 discard leading 1: 752

3
    (i)   6/19 = 0.315789473 ...   (ii)   n/9 (0 < n < 10) = 0.nnnnnn ...

Divided by 2		6
Remainder		**Quotient**
0	3	
1	1	
1	5	
1	7	
1	8	
0	9	
1	4	
0	7	
1	3	

Divided by 1		n
Remainder		**Quotient**
0	n	
0	n	
0	n	
0	n	
0	n	
0	n	
0	n	
0	n	
0	n	

4.

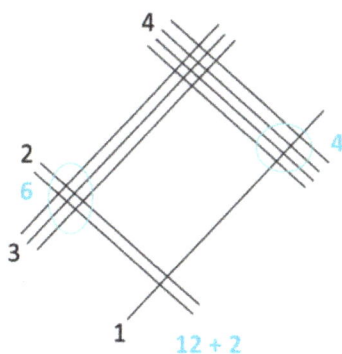

Result 744

139

5. Russian Peasant Method: 23 x 49

23	49	
46	24	ignore
92	12	ignore
184	6	ignore
368	3	
736	1	736 + 368 +23 = 1127

6.

187	Rem
93	1
46	1
23	0
11	1
5	1
2	1
1	0
0	1

Result 10111011

7.

512	256	128	64	32	16	8	4	2	1
1	0	1	1	0	1	1	0	0	1

8.

$$\frac{108 \text{ pence}}{\text{litre}} \times \frac{1 \text{ Litre}}{1.75 \text{ pints}} \times \frac{8 \text{ pints}}{1 \text{ gallon}} \times \frac{\pounds 1}{100 \text{ pence}} = \frac{108 \times 1 \times 8 \times 1 \pounds}{1.75 \times 1 \times 100 \text{ pence}} = \frac{\pounds 864}{175 \text{ gallons}}$$

Result: 108 pence per litre = £4.94 per gallon

9.   1, 3, 4, 7, 11, 18, 29, 47, 76, 123   29 x 11 = 319

10.   153 x 11   Copy the first digit: 1
                        Add the first and second digits: 1 + 5 = 6
                        Add the second and third digits: 5 + 3 = 8
                        Copy the last digit: 3
                        Write down the result: 1683

A Few Parting Words

I hope that you have enjoyed this collection. I realise that some parts are more difficult than others, but I hope that you persevered with the trickier bits. If there were some topics that you didn't tackle, do try and come back to them at a later date.

When I chose the material for this book, I was looking for topics with a slightly quirky appeal. It was such things that first made me interested in mathematics and made me wish that I had become involved many years before.

Some of the subject matter is of an advanced nature, but I think that the basic ideas can grasped with a little effort and I have tried to present these in a form that doesn't require previous knowledge.

Never be afraid to ask questions! When I was a student and the lecturer was presenting a baffling explanation of some complicated theory, I would look around at my fellow students who were all nodding wisely and appeared to be having no difficulty. Feeling slightly foolish, I would ask a question explaining my difficulty in an attempt to understand the topic and, usually, the explanation would make things much clearer. It was only after the lecture that my fellow students would say "I'm so glad that you asked that question because I was totally confused!"

Similarly, there is much to be said for sharing your enthusiasm with your friends. If you have found something interesting it is quite natural to want to share it and by doing so, you will often get some feedback that might advance your own knowledge.

By the same token, I welcome your comments on this book and if this involves constructive criticism, then so much the better. Any communication should be through the publisher using the e-mail: mathspuzzles@takahepublishing.co.uk

Thank you for the considerable time and effort that you have put in engaging with this book and I hope that this has been a useful experience. More importantly, It is my hope that this may have inspired you to engage with mathematical and related topics.

I would just like to finish on a note regarding a former university lecturer colleague. We were having lunch and he asked me what I thought about a particular issue. I replied "Well, I have no interest in the matter". This most knowledgeable man and highly respected academic firmly put me in my place by replying somewhat crossly, "You should be interested in everything!" I have often reflected on that encounter and concluded that he was right! If I can pass on to you those words, then I shall feel that I have done something worthwhile!

www.ingramcontent.com/pod-product-compliance
Lightning Source LLC
Chambersburg PA
CBHW050257090426
42734CB00022B/3479

9 781908 837035